"A man who has never gone to school may steal a freight car; but if he has a university education, he may steal the whole railroad."
- **Theodore Roosevelt**

U-N-I-VERSE 3
THE SYSTEM

BY
S. LITTLE & G. HOPKINS

Forward

When I look at the Universe (Sun, Moon and Stars) I see something that is missing in humanity. That element - which is null and void - would provide a blueprint for us to follow that would propel the human families in the immediate direction of success.

That which I recognize in the Universe can be found the word itself. Let me establish, before I proceed, that the Physical Universe that we all see, live in, and submit to consist of the Sun, Moon, Stars and all that exist in between.

The Term "Universe" is made up of a prefix (Uni) and a single word (Verse). Prefix means before and "Uni" means "One". While "Verse" is another term for "Word". Now when you look at the word "Uni-Verse" as a sum of its parts you have "One-Word" and that "One Word" is to "Be". "Be" means "to exist (in a form of I Study Life Around Me (Islam))."

The Universe was set in place to remind us to become one and/or exist as "One" under the banner of Islam.

Upon further investigation I was able to dissect the word even further, by breaking it down into sections and manifesting a paralleling between us and that which seems to be *"Out-of-this-world"* in a manner of speaking.

So, when I assayed the word Universe, I came up with U-N-I-Verse - meaning; "You and I Verse or Versus" and it added much more substance to the above said meaning. Where You and I (U-N-I) must become one; we have to unite in order to exist and verse the devil's uncivilized and wicked machinations, both mentally and physically.

- George Hopkins

Preface

"Then Pharaoh gave this order to all his people: "Every Hebrew boy that is born you must throw into the Nile, but let every girl live." -Exodus 1:22

When Herod realized that he had been outwitted by the Magi, he was furious, and he gave orders to kill all the boys in Bethlehem and its vicinity who were two years old and under, in accordance with the time he had learned from the Magi." -Matthew 2:16

As with all things discussed, we should dive into the definition of that which we begin to elucidate and expound upon. Merriam-Webster dictionary defines "system" in the following way:

1: a regularly interacting or interdependent group of items forming a unified whole

2: an organized set of doctrines, ideas, or principles usually intended to explain the arrangement or working of a systematic whole

3a: an organized or established procedure

 b: a manner of classifying, symbolizing, or schematizing

4: harmonious arrangement or pattern: ORDER

5: an organized society or social situation regarded as stultifying or oppressive: **ESTABLISHMENT** *—usually used with* **the**

When we speak of "The System" we are speaking in particular of the prison industrial complex and those "systems" that serve as extensions thereof. I refer in particular to the matrix (a system within which a "thing" is conditioned i.e., definitions 2 and 5 above working in congruence) that leads one to the final destination which would be the prison system in this particular treatise. However, knowledge of and defense against the health system, spiritual system, racial system, religious system, psychological system, etc. that lead one to the prison system are as integral if not more so than the ending they lead to.

In modern times, the ubiquitous presence of technology, in particular, cameras, humans have been forced to view the corruption that for so many years went unnoticed and unreported. A reflection of this can be seen in the recent sense of urgency at which citizens and policy-makers are pushing for prison reform. The criminalization, or rather, the decriminalization of marijuana being another act of atoning for overt hypocrisy within each branch of legislation - Judicial, Executive and Legislative. What becomes even more apparent as we face these universal mirrors is there is and has always been a system in place to disguise this hypocrisy which affected the lives of millions and billions of minorities worldwide.

In the scriptures of the three Abrahamic faiths, emphasis is placed on the story of Moses and Pharoah. Rightfully so. The story is densely packed with spiritual jewelry. What will be extracted for the use of this introduction is the system in which Pharaoh created to enslave whom he felt to be an inferior people, his obsession with the destruction of male children, and his fear of equality compromising the status he coveted.

In the Holy Quran he advises his subjects to be wary of Moosa (Moses) and Harun (Aaron) for their intent was to *"Destroy their lovely institutions."* Hence, anything which opposes the system, its ideologies, aims and protocols must be totally disregarded and terminated if it becomes too threatening to the establishment and its institutions. When the threat becomes imminent, he begins to order the murdering of male children. This is done up until this day.

The modern Pharaoh has instituted a system that aims to destroy minority children, male children in particular, from birth and before so. Contraceptives. They become necessary in a society overwhelmed by lust, desire, and sexual promiscuity and deviance. Still, the aim is the control of birth and ultimately population control. Poison foods are introduced to the embryo early in development and usually become the staple diet throughout the child's life. There is always the massive assault on the ideas and overall psyche of the child by the media. Innocent children are introduced to environments that teach them to prey or be preyed upon. Often, they are eaten before they even grow the teeth to bite back. If the mother is uncultivated, she can be utilized to destroy the child's credit before it ever learns what credit is.

It becomes equally important to keep the slave working massive amounts of hours so as to materialize what vision the modern Pharaoh chooses to finance with the resources, he's stolen from the very slaves doing his bidding. This gives rise to what William Cooper coined "Occupational Orphans" - children who have parents but are orphans in essence because they rarely see their parents due to work. These children are raised by teenagers, daycares, TVs, Video Games, and almost everything and everyone other than the man and woman through whom they came. Hence a divide begins because the matrix indoctrinating the child may not be identical to the one that programmed the parent hence, they become strangers. As strangers to each other, inconsiderate of the other's feelings due to a lack of understanding predicated on an inability to associate with and relate to the other's nuances, they argue, fight, and in some cases, kill each other.

By adolescence, if the parents haven't escaped the system that destroys children (medical, dietary, public school, TV and radio programming, etc.) the child has already begun to make its way towards the prison system. Inside, this child, mostly male children (In Pennsylvania there is one female state prison to 30+ male prisons), will be further indoctrinated by and engrained to a self-destructive system or he will become aware of those systems which have led to his downfall and creates on for himself that will lead to his eventual rising from the grave. Peace.

-Saleem Little

*"The more corrupt the state, the more
numerous the laws."*
- Tacitus

CHAPTER 1

Covid-19's Impact
on People in Prison
by Saleem Little

"*People who are incarcerated are at great risk of sickness and death as a result of the Covid-19 pandemic and more must be done to release people who are imprisoned and are not a threat to public safety or are elderly or infirm. The inability to quarantine or practice social distancing, together with overcrowding, imperils the lives of many people incarcerated in jails and prisons.*"

-Equal Justice Initiative.org (April 2021)

One can only imagine that if the suggested preventive measure against the Covid-19 virus is *"social distancing"*, a place like a prison would be one of the hardest places to prevent the spread of the disease. According to research, this seems to be the case. Inmates are infected by the coronavirus at a reported rate of more than five times higher than the nation's overall rate and according to a report in the *Journal of the American Medical Association* (July 2020), The reported death rate of inmates which is approximately 39 deaths per 100,000 inmates is also much higher than the national rate of 29 deaths per 100,000 people.

Since what can be traced as the beginning of the outbreak and up until as recent as April 16th (2021) an excess of 661,000 incarcerated people and Department of Corrections staff members have been infected with the virus with as many as 2,990 dying from complications associated with Covid.* The issue with the reported numbers and the accuracy or revelation thereof is the number of infections and deaths is actually more likely to be higher than what is reported when you take into consideration the unsettling realities that many jails and prisons are conducting very limited testing on inmates and many facilities won't even test incarcerated individuals who die after showing symptoms of the Covid-19 virus.

As stated, one would expect for a facility where people are being held against their will - albeit for infractions they may have committed against the communities in which they live and society in general - would be high on the list of highly transmittable environments and according to *The New York Times*, prisons in America *"have been among the nation's most dangerous places when it comes to infections from the coronavirus...Over the past year, more than 1,400 new inmate infections and seven deaths, on average, have been reported inside those facilities each day."*

One in three people incarcerated in state prisons are known to have had Covid-19, *The Times* reported. At least 39% of people held in federal facilities are known to have been infected, according to the same publication. Hence this pandemic has also highlighted problems within the Department of Corrections and Prison Industrial Complex in general that need to be assessed and addressed more aggressively in the very near future. The most obvious of these issues is the problem of *Overcrowding.*

With the explosion of arrest for petty crimes often more corrigible through counseling, addiction recovery retreats, and trade schools, prisons in the United States now have many more people incarcerated within them than they were designed to house. Because of this overcrowding, the federal Bureau of

Prisons had a total number of prisoners in custody that either met or exceeded the minimum number of beds needed. This has led to many inmates being crammed into dorms and warehoused in rooms with bunks sometimes three beds high and only inches apart. Obviously, under immensely crowded and overpacked conditions social distancing of any sort is next to impossible, even laughable and because of this impossibility to quarantine large numbers of infected prisoners, the risk of infection is higher than the national averages.

After decades of extreme sentencing, older adults today make up a larger share of the state prison population than people age 18 to 24. Older people are at a higher risk of serious complications from Covid-19. Older people in prison are more likely to be in poor health and have limited access to quality medical services, which increases the risk of death in a public health crisis.

"Tough on crime" policies including three-strikes laws and truth-in-sentencing schemes have dramatically increased sentences for people convicted of felonies and significantly reduced eligibility for parole. Accordingly, the percentage of people in state prisons who are 55 and older more than tripled

between 2000 and 2016—to nearly 150,000 older people incarcerated in state correctional facilities in 2016.

-EJI (Equal Justice Initiative.org)

There has also been a decrease in staff which can be viewed as a catalyst in the spike of violence that has transpired in the prisons due to the pandemic. The need to reduce inmates has been a pressing issue for quite some time now but the pandemic has highlighted and intensified the need to do so. County jails are full of prisoners who may or may not be convicted of a crime but can't afford bail leaving hundreds of potentially innocent men and women at risk to infection or the spreading thereof. Advocates, family members, and prosecutors called for jails and prisons to release the most vulnerable people, especially the elderly and infirm, who are at the greatest risk from Covid-19, yet and still a lot more must be done to make this a reality as it this has now become a life-or-death situation in the most literal sense.

"Over the past year, "lawmakers failed to reduce prison and jail populations enough to slow down the spread of the coronavirus," the Prison Policy Initiative found, "causing incarcerated

people to get sick and die at a rate unparalleled in the general public."

-Prison Policy Initiative

Sources:
The American Medical Journal
The New York Times
Prison Policy Initiative

"Corrupt politicians make the other ten percent look bad."
- Henry Kissinger

CHAPTER 2

Interview
w/ George Hopkins & Saleem Little

1. (Saleem Little) How did the Covid-19 pandemic affect prisons and prisoners? What type of research, info and plans have been presented to inmates in regards to the virus and vaccinations?

Answer: (George Hopkins) The Covid-19 Pandemic was very detrimental, stressful and enervating for the men trapped behind these walls. Initially, it was looked at as a virus that couldn't - or wouldn't - affect the black population, so very little concern was given to the pandemic. I believe everyone incarcerated watched the news - as the D.O.C. (Department of Corrections.) was immediately locked down when traces of the virus were detected in the prisons.

I personally started to pay attention more when billion-dollar corporations began to shut down their businesses i.e., *March Madness* (Colleges and Universities) and the NBA, that was when I knew it was real!

The pandemic affected us on many different planes of existence and I will try my best to vividly explain the horrors we have been experiencing.

The Covid-19 pandemic that terrorized the nation equally paralyzed the Pennsylvania State Prison System. The best way to explain this is to say, if you can remember how the country was shut down, then take that and magnify our situation by ten! We literally were forced into solitary confinement - as all movement was ceased.

We no longer were allowed outside our cells, and being confined in a space no bigger than the bathroom of the person reading this - with another man and/or woman for five hundred and forty-five days straight has a way of eroding the potency of the one thing that keeps one sane - our minds! So, we were afforded no recreational activity: working out, sports, or just having the luxury of breathing fresh air and feeling the rays of the sun's light. Every educational, drug or rehabilitative program was halted, and for a group of people who are already deficient in these areas, this crippled us even more. The walls got even tighter, so suffocating, that I myself wished to have more than one set of arms to act as pillars to keep them at bay.

Along with this was the fact that we were being rived of our weekly sanctuary at the chapel - as this is probably the most important day to a believer - besides his or her release date.

The social environment that we enjoyed amongst each other - and is vital for one to keep his screws tight - was suddenly no more.

As I think back, and remember the chilling discovery of how or why the TV is teen suicide rate has skyrocketed during the pandemic, which at the time I could not understand oh, I now comprehend it. Just knowing that we, meaning people in general, are social beings, and when that element is stripped, a part of who we are is taken as well. And that leads to depression or at the highest-level suicide. I, personally, can identify with that. There were many days I awoke in a depressed state thinking to myself should I give up? Or, what's the use of living anymore? That atmosphere is hard to escape when there is no escape.

Imprison we can only obtain sagacity from playing off of each other's personal experiences to deal with, or figure out, our own problems.

To add on to the social nutrients one needs to feed their mental, emotional and spiritual well-being is our visitation with our families. This too was and is an element that has been carved out of our lives. Try to imagine a gregarious person - which we all are by nature - being deprived of human contact - not being able to touch, hold, kiss, sit face to face with, laugh or talk with your parents, siblings, children, grandchildren, wife, girlfriend, etc. these types of actions literally harden the heart, turns one savage and debilitates the spirit of a person.

The flipside is that the department of corrections during this time was able to machinate new articles of oppression for us under the guise of safety and security. What this means is they are using the safety and security of guards - and supposedly inmates - as the reason why these extreme measures are being enforced. Yet and still, violence is still an eminent element within the jail as I am writing this. So, before the pandemic, we were afforded the opportunity to eat breakfast, lunch and dinner in a chow hall amongst other inmates, but due to the virus and subsequent lock down, we all had to eat in our cells, which is understandable when you take into consideration the severity of what was going on globally.

Now that the pandemic is clearing up, this new rule of eating in our cells is still being enforced. In fact, it is being said that we'll never be able to eat in the chow hall again. Which, if viewed properly, is another way of secluding and isolating the population. It's all about control with the D.O.C. and any way they can figure out how to apply pressure to our necks with the heel of their boots they will.

Let me double back to the visitations for a minute and give you another one of their machinated schemes. During the pandemic, the D.O.C. afforded us virtual visits with our families and in some schools of thought, that may have been looked upon as a blessing but let me show you why it is now being used as a curse.

For some strange reason the D.O.C. has criminalized our families and seems to believe that our hard-working, law-abiding family members would risk their freedom to bring drugs into the facility through the visitation room. (This does happen but the amount of drugs brought in by family members are no larger than the amounts brought in by staff members and both have been easily containable for decades). So, now the idea of Virtual visits versus Contact visits is being tossed around in administrative offices under the "Safety & Security" protocol because it is perceived or falsely projected - that the elimination of contact visits would be beneficial for safety and security but not too detrimental because we now have the virtual visits.

Now, for a place that promotes family contact as a means to remain civilized and a part of our rehabilitative process, it would literally go against their mission statement altogether, and create such an inhuman atmosphere within these walls that very few - next to none would recover.

As far as the information we were given in regards to Covid, most - if not all - of the information we received came from the news media outlets. However, at my jail (SCI-GREENE), we had a weekly Town Hall show that aired throughout the prison. On this channel, we were taught the importance of cleanliness, how the virus attacks the body, how it is contracted and we were given free medical checkups.

1. What are the physical effects of separation from loved ones? Does this affect the spiritual connection as well?

GH: The physical effects of separation from loved ones goes unnoticed by the untrained eye, but those who have an iota of consciousness can see and feel the manifestations of separation. Science says, "For every cause there is an equal and opposite effect." When one is separated from the natural way of life - which is man, woman and child - a natural regression takes place that stifles our growth so much that things one wouldn't normally do become a reflex of coping mechanisms.

There is drug abuse that helps one escape the realities of this separation and a variety of medications used to remove the abstract element of existence. It numbs the pain of not being able to grow with our family in a civilized environment. The usage of e-cigarettes is the new thing to assist with the pain, stress and loneliness of being isolated from our loved ones. All of these addictive behaviors that we employ to relieve the anguish of the 13th Amendment destroys our physical makeup, turning us into *suicide bombers* against self and others.

The withdrawal from the connection of family has a way of tearing our hearts apart - to the point where one can become cold-hearted and this effect is so stressful that some develop eating disorders, either becoming anorexic or obese. Some don't go to the yard, due to the depression that forms internally. That dearth of Vitamin D (sunlight) that would naturally give light, life and power; feeding the brain and body, causes a depletion to the physical attributes and eventually one begins to look pale, old and wrinkled; decrepit even.

In fact, it does affect the spiritual connection with himself, family and God as one tends to die inside, becomes a shell of himself, and no longer cares about how they look so their upkeep will become unkempt, whether or not their cell is clean, or even if they took a shower. It is so easy to lose all hope and when the bridge to the Most-High is instantly snatched away a Kamikaze response, coping mechanism, and reflex. And while family may care, love, support and harbor deep concern to the individual it is just him or her there and that this connection deteriorates the spirit into a rehabilitation is an afterthought if that.

This particular question is exceptional as this may be one of the main reasons why so many people - 70% - are repeat offenders. I mean, where one may possibly be a success story if given the proper tools, i.e., a good job, better education, and more positive outlets. Instead, we are sentenced to prison because of the lack thereof (skills, trades and guidance) and pronounced incorrigible. Then we are treated inhumane and those two factors; being treated inhumane and separated from family, quickly changes our perception to that of a Savage. And if we are lucky enough to make parole three to four years after our minimum, we are expected to act civilized. Now of course this does not apply to the whole prison population because there are many that make it.

1. Please expound upon the importance of mail and the therapeutic nature of both sending and receiving.
Answer: when a person is afforded the blessing of hearing their name called for mail an internal thought of elation that probably goes unnoticed to all emerges that says, *"I am important to my family…"* or, *"My family does love me."* those that do not have that luxury feel the reverse effect. Again, it is so subtle that it isn't easily detectable. Seeing as though love is an action word, we

"unconsciously" tie that action (love), or the lack thereof to the receiving a mail.

"Love", which is a verb or action, has to be linked to an act of doing something. That something is allotting time (which some claim is impossible in today's fast-paced society) to write a letter.

Being as though writing is an art, the therapy a prisoner gets when he or she sits down to write a letter to someone special is immense. It allows for a release of the impurities frequently unseen within our spirit. Sometimes things are hard to say over the phone, or in person, but when writing, it is just you and the pen. That's why diaries are very beneficial to the person and their spirit. So, we use the receiver of our mail as our personal diaries.

When we receive mail from the outside world, knowing that a person manipulated their time schedule to show some love it brightens our day and eases the everyday stress of being in prison. It also keeps us in tune with the everyday happenings of that person and the world. Which gives us the opportunity to not be too lost when we step back outside of these gates. As the recipient of mail, we not only become our loved one's personal diary -

which I myself embrace wholeheartedly, but also, we unknowingly - with no educational background take on the role of a therapist/psychologist as we listen and try to administer remedies to the problems, stress and pain our family devolves to us. In turn, that helps us to solve some of our own problems, but more importantly, it gives us a sense of purpose to those who otherwise feel useless.

1. In your confinement, I'm sure you've discovered the deficiencies in the systems created by society that lead a child to a life of crime and subsequently incarceration. I'm sure you've also discovered internal deficiencies that have nothing to do with external factors. Maybe the two are inseparable. Please reveal what you've discovered in regards to what we call in psychology "The Imprint Stage" and how individuals fail society, and vice versa.

Answer: in dealing with the "Imprint stage" and how it affects a person throughout their lifetime, we first must know what that means. According to the New World Collegiate Webster's dictionary, imprinting is described as *"a learning mechanism operating very early in the life of an animal, in which a particular stimulus immediately establishes an irreversible behavior pattern with reference to the same stimulus in the future."*

In short, we imprint, or train (indoctrinate even) the child to an exclusive minutiae way of thinking. This chains the individual to a box they cannot think outside of. So, the saying goes, *"The person who gives you your diameter of knowledge controls your circumference of thinking."*

This process "Imprint Stage" has been one of the main intrinsic reasons why our society - and the world - as a whole is trending in the wrong direction. Imprinting to me - whether it is religion, politics, racism, music, morals, values, etc. - is the planting of a seed, and we all plant seeds - whether good or bad. The thinking about a seed is that even if it hasn't taken root yet, it is still alive - though it remains in a dormant stage until it gets watered. Our children are so impressionable, eager to learn by emulation that they soak in every iota of information afforded to them. This in turn creates what we see today - a world in shambles.

Take for instance movies like *"Boys in da Hood"*, *"Menace II Society"*, *"Juice"*, etc. and how the black man is portrayed in each production. That image - or seed - is planted or imprinted in the minds of the American people to the point where we - young black men - take on these roles in real life. Look at the murder rate in the predominantly black communities throughout America. It is heartbreaking!

I personally think that this is what happened - a prime example - to Tupac Shakur. A beautiful talent, and so much more, began acting out the roles he played in movies, i.e., "Juice" in real life. So, he became Bishop and couldn't turn it off. More revealing is that a new terminology has emerged among inner city youth, "Shooting a Movie", a description of a violent or debaucherously excessive scene about to play out in real life.

The flipside to these Hollywood made films is how white America views us: as unintelligent, incorrigible, menaces, niggas, savages and one of the most distasteful - "Super Predator" -a term used to describe inner city blacks by the same woman who courted the *black vote* in 2016.

Why is any of this important? Because when you look at the other side of the spectrum, Hollywood almost always portrays the Caucasian man as an upstanding citizen, a good father, one who worlds or has a business of some sort, a police officer, judge or president.

These images are stamped in our subconscious so well that the movie screen is now being reenacted in our everyday lives. We do a disservice to humanity by painting these images, by promoting the success of one group of people and simultaneously destroying the other. So, we fail society every second in the day we choose not to uplift our neighbor. The lending of a helping hand is so microscopic that it will go unnoticed to everyone outside of the act, but has enough power/love to reverse the polarities of someone's life. The old adage: "It takes a village to raise a child" has never been truer and should be employed more often. I will leave it there for now as this is a subject that volumes of books could be written on.

1. For one who may be health-conscious, how hard is it to maintain a healthy regiment in prison?

Answer: being healthy in prison is not easy. We are only supplied with a limited amount of food on our trays - a portion so small that a first grader would be hard-pressed to find satisfaction. We're afforded only enough to keep us alive.

The quality of the food is so low probably a grade C or D - that any nutrients or protein it contains is most likely left in the pot while being transported to our trays. The food is so nasty, and sometimes even smells bad or may not be thoroughly cooked that some who are fortunate enough to afford commissary isn't much healthier - as it is filled with snacks and the food is prepackaged, processed and saturated with sodium. Not to mention the taxing of our pockets. So, one has to literally pick their poison: commissary or prison food. So, being healthy in prison - physically as well as mentally - is an afterthought.

1. Now that more and more technology is being permitted to inmates, have you noticed a decline in reading?

Answer: There has always been a decline in reading. To most people, it is outdated and obsolete; boring and lacks animation. With the advent of the technological devices in prison, the short attention spans of the inmates are now being occupied with little to no effort. My personal opinion is that these items were introduced to keep the population content, docile, and to dumb us down by keeping us away from books, the law library and other therapeutic programs. It's sad because if a magazine or book doesn't have any pictures, especially of women, then they are not being touched. Again, I believe this is the plan, the dumbing down of inmates because the more we read and learn, the less likely it is that we'll continue on a path to destruction.

Ultimately, that would take money out of the DOC's pockets. The evidence to my claim can be proven in the fact that at one point in time, we were allowed to get degrees from college while being incarcerated. That can no longer happen, even within the prison there were vocational programs afforded, now there are next to none available and or they are so hard to get into that most don't even attempt to apply.

So, again, it is all a part of the process of making sure we come back to put food on their table and creating an environment where reading is not even an afterthought is paramount to this success.

I would like to thank you for this opportunity and questionnaire. Peace and blessings to all.

-George Hopkins 2021

"Dear Government... I'm going to have a serious talk with you if I ever find anyone to talk to."
- Stieg Larsson

CHAPTER 3

Govern-ment
By Saleem Little

Politically institutionalized Governments are the result of people's inability to govern themselves. The irony of the government is that the people who complain of its dominance are direct beneficiaries of its policies i.e., welfare, Medicaid, Section 8, child support, stimulus aid, etc. It's hypocritical to complain about a government's authority when it is essentially your own laziness that keeps it in existence.

A parent realizes a child is dependent upon them and so along with providing, rules are stipulated that must be obeyed to secure future benefits. It is no different with the government. If you want welfare, you must make sure the father does no more than visit your apartment.
If you get a vasectomy, you can be rewarded further.

The same is to be said of the medical industry. It thrives because people are, in essence, too lazy and lack the discipline to heal themselves. So, the act of healing is now big business. Often, shallow people will brag about their position in the medical field. What they are alluding to is their financial bracket, not a desire to heal people for there rarely is any real desire or passion to do so. Many employees of the medical industry don't care for their own health, let alone a stranger's. How confusing is it to see a doctor or Physician, the person responsible for advising you on health, smoking cigarettes on break? For the conscious, there is an awkwardness in being cared for by an obese nurse. This is not a judgement upon a person's flaws in regards to health rather an investigation into motives and intentions.

On numerous occasions I've received praise for my health by physicians who openly loathed their own. I could spend years exchanging simple thoughts for words and then those simple words for more complex words in pursuit of a degree for my wall and abbreviation for my name, this would indeed increase my earning potential. It is, however, no indictment on my health as much as it is a reflection of my knowledge of health. It has no bearing on my ethics. More often than not, college students base their career choice on salary projections and industry health. Hence some Doctors, Nurses, Officers, Psychologists and Psychiatrists steal, cheat, lie, and commit the same infractions associated with a lack of spiritual cultivation as the lay person.

A shallow world full of shallow pursuits. Shallow minds are hollow and in need of governing to feel the empty space that leads to straying. Hence, this particular system is actually the creation of the oppressed not the oppressor. You're born free. At some point, somehow and in some way, you forfeit this freedom and a system is created to control the slave you've become.

He or she who will not rule the self will be ruled by the self of another. External forces will always be in control and the human will become a mule that is ridden until it dies or can be ridden no more. Choosing to be a slave to desire makes one the slave of men and women. He or she will be enslaved to men or women for material gain, sexual desire and every other desire that requires an external exponent to satiate, or, satisfy it. One can expect nothing but slavery until the characteristics of freedom are manifested.

ר֫וּחַ אֲדֹנָ֤י יֱהֹוִה֙ עָלָ֔י יַ֛עַן מָשַׁ֨ח יְהֹוָ֥ה אֹתִ֜י לְבַשֵּׂ֣ר עֲנָוִ֗ים שְׁלָחַ֙נִי֙ לַחֲבֹ֣שׁ לְנִשְׁבְּרֵי־לֵ֔ב לִקְרֹ֤א לִשְׁבוּיִם֙ דְּר֔וֹר וְלַאֲסוּרִ֖ים פְּקַח־קֽוֹחַ׃

"The Spirit of the Lord Yah-weh is upon
me, Because Yah-weh has anointed me to
bring good news to the afflicted; He
has sent me to
bind up the brokenhearted, to proclaim
liberty to captives and freedom to
prisoners."
-Isaiah 61:1

CHAPTER 4

An open letter
By Anonymous

Your life is not fully in your control. No matter how many people try to persuade you otherwise. Right now, your life is in the hands of the beast. I awoke today full of hope and optimism. I arose early like a bird but returned to the nest empty-handed. I went to get a job today. The lady all but said *"No"*.

"Most of our clients don't care how old the felony is, they don't accept felons…"

That was my cue. A few weeks prior a Caregiving service had said something similar and gave me the runaround for weeks. They stalled my hiring process, eliminated the possibility of working with them on any level other than Customer Direct, which would have been direct care of a particular family member who had a stroke a few years prior.

At twenty I allowed myself to be indicted in a crime by associating with my "friends" from the neighborhood. At forty I still suffer the repercussions.

Everything else is closed now (due to Covid-19) so it doesn't make much sense to entertain hope. Our grandparents failed our parents and our parents failed us. In turn, we have already begun to fail the next generation. Now, all we can do is watch the destruction of society.

At first there's pain, then there's numbness. I've been rejected so many times I can't count, prejudged more times than I can recall. If I remind myself daily that I'm a black man and an ex-con I don't expect much. It's when I forget what people think by lying to myself that it doesn't matter (what your potential employer, partner, etc. thinks of you most definitely matters); when I concern myself solely with how I view myself and how "The One" views me that I leave my threshold full of joy and ambition. In this forgetful state, I suffer the frequent insulting reminder (instead of silently reminding myself) of my social status and suffer disappointment. I don't believe the solution is self-hatred, just acceptance…

43

*"Power attracts the corruptible.
Suspect any who seek it."*
- Frank Herbert

CHAPTER 5

**The effects of Covid-19
on the Religious System**
by Saleem Little

*The Prophet got up from his sleep with
a flushed red face and said, "None has
the right to be worshipped but Allah.
Woe to the Arabs, from the Great evil
that is nearly approaching them. Today
a gap has been made in the wall of Gog
and Magog like this." (Sufyan
illustrated by forming the number 90 or
100 with his fingers.) It was asked,
"Shall we be destroyed though there are
righteous people among us?" The Prophet
said, "Yes, if evil increased."*

Narrated Zainab bint Jahsh:
Reference: Sahih al-Bukhari 7059, Bk.
92, Hadith 11

It was a Friday afternoon in Steelton, Pennsylvania, a small borough outside of Harrisburg with a population of about. Although it was September it was noticeably warm for this time of year. I was preparing to enter the Jumu'ah service at a local mosque when I was immediately transported from that sacred mental plane to the profane world in which all exist. The doors had signs forbidding entrance without a mask covering. Inside, the name of Allah was barely visible as the posters for vaccinations covered the walls. Slowly, more and more believers began to file in, nowhere near as many as usual for such a large masjid, and all wore masks. Majority of the men brought personal prayer rugs because they would be practicing social distancing during salaat (prayer). I could no longer focus on anything holy, righteous or meditative, I simply could not stop scanning the posters of needles and masks. Had the pandemic invaded the spiritual world as well?

The Arabs of the desert are the worst in Unbelief and hypocrisy, and most fitted to be in ignorance of the command which Allah hath sent down to His Messenger: But Allah is All-knowing, All-Wise.

-Holy Quran Sharrief 9:97

In 2020, Hajj was limited to 1,000 locals and foreigners living in the kingdom. In 2021, Saudi King Salman announced there would be no such limits. However, this did not mean the hajj would return to normal. This sacred act that is seen as an obligation for the 1.6 billion devout followers of the Prophet Muhammad, believers in the One God, and submitters to Islam, was now being hampered by a material hinderance and compromised by authorities.

The Saudi Arabia Health Ministry mandated Covid-19 Vaccinations and announced they would be mandatory for all pilgrims wishing to make the annual hajj (pilgrimage) to Mecca; the holiest city in Islamic tradition. Participants in both, the major *hajj* and lesser *umrah*, would be required to show proof of vaccination before being allowed to participate in the rituals.

The overseers of Mecca wasted no time signing off on vaccines that were and still are in experimental phases, i.e., *Moderna*, *Pfizer* and *AstraZeneca*. Officials began injecting Meccans in December.

> **Abu Huraira reported: The Prophet, peace and blessing be upon him, said, "Woe to the rulers! Woe to the chiefs! Woe to the trustees! Some people will wish on the Day of Resurrection that their hair was hanging from the sky and swinging between heaven and earth, rather than to have done anything they did."**

Source: Musnad Ahmad 8627

Because of deals made long ago, Saudi Arabia is in partnerships with Western countries and more often than not, not in the position to question mandates that are passed down from the head of the pyramid. Mecca, once considered to be one of, if no thee, holiest city on this six-sextillion ton globe covering 196, 940, 000 square miles of space, is engaged in the unholiest of geopolitical relationships with Washington D.C. and a major supplier of planes, guns, ammunition and weapons of destructions that are used against other Muslim nations.

At this point the once holy city of Mecca is experiencing desolation and ungodly abominations foretold in hadith but unnoticed by the trained eye. Many believe in prophecy; few see it's unfolding. Engaging in the bombing of Yemen and Shiite in Iran in accordance with the policies who are open enemies to the very faith all Muslims, regardless of sect, cherish and strive to submit to.

Covid-19 has had an effect and impact on the economy of Mecca as well. Hajj generates approximately $1.2 billion annually. At eight percent of the

Kingdom's GNP, 1.9 million inhabitants suffered unemployment.

With health care officials aiding the pilgrims, these devotees are no longer allowed to touch the *Kaaba,* let alone kiss the black stone which incited *takbir* (professing God's greatness) in the prophet and tears in the eyes of countless hopefuls.

It was narrated that 'Umar (may Allah be pleased with him) came to the Black Stone and kissed it, then he said: "I know that you are only a stone which can neither bring benefit nor cause harm. Were it not that I had seen the Prophet (peace and blessings of Allah be upon him) kiss you, I would not have kissed you." Narrated by al-Bukhari, 1520; Muslim, 1720

"When one gets in bed with government, one must expect the diseases it spreads."
- Ron Paul

CHAPTER 6

The Incredible Hulk
By George Hopkins

T.V.
Movies
Hollywood
The Powers that be

The **10%** they control all the major systems in America. These major systems are seven in number and are as follows:

- The Legal System
- The Religious System
- The Educational System
- The Political System
- The Economic System
- The Military

- ***Entertainment***

"Entertainment" is an essential element because of its *"Long Arms"* - or - ability to reach everyone on the planet. And this is how messages, information, news and other viable things are passed along to us.

Jay-Z once made the erroneous statement, *"it's only entertainment"*, when speaking about music, but he was sadly mistaken.

Being as though we think *"it's only entertainment"* we miss the hidden message in the television shows and movies we watch. This is because of the entertainment aspect that we're so enthralled with.

The incredible Hulk was just a mere man, up until an experiment went wrong. This botched experiment affected him immensely, and then he became a danger to all! He walked around in society as a normal Human Being. He worked, he ate regular food, he paid bills, etc., but any time he got excited/or agitated and especially angry/or mad, he would turn to the "Hulk"- A giant green, angry, overbearing muscular ball of fire with one purpose in mind- destroy- or how he eloquently labeled it –

"SMASH!"

It's not hard to see (if you're familiar with the character) that the Hulk had anger issues, and throughout his life of living with the side effects of an experiment gone bad; he tried to develop different ways to handle, manage and strive with his dis-ease (disease). He moved away from confrontation and the inner city- mainly because the government was out to obtain him. He also learned meditation and different breathing techniques to assist in curving his attitude problem. While some of these things worked, it was but for a short time. To the Hulk healing seemed impossible. There was only one thing that could calm him - a woman.

She was the only one that could tame the beast. Her eyes, her smile, her look; her touch, her smell, her taste; her voice, her comfort, her compassion, her understanding, her femininity, her - essence, her everything!

Once in the form of the Hulk nothing could stop him - not even bullets, bombs, or the army, but she was able to bring "Peace and Serenity" to an otherwise lost incorrigible person. There is a catch however. Not just any woman could precipitate this effect and while she was a key component in the Hulk's rehabilitation, the main ingredient was the "Love" that radiated between the two of them. This shows and proves that "Love" is the only element capable of saving the planet; and therefore, an individual who has nothing to live for.

Need I say more?

CHAPTER 7

Revolutionized
By Saleem Little

"This is blatant racism!" my attorney blurted out. I was amazed at how defensive she had become in regards to, not only my case, but my welfare. I suppose the many talks with my mother had spurned maternal instincts even a career in cruel litigations couldn't eradicate.

"What did you say?!" the judge shot back.

He had dropped his glasses and cast a cold stare at my Defense Attorney. It was a stare that made even me shutter. My attorney hadn't backed down, though her voice did crack subtly from nervousness as she responded.

"My client, a black man, is being sentenced to 5-10 years while his co-defendants, two white women, are guilty of the same crime, yet you sentenced them to four years of probation..."

"Well, your client also has a prior record..."

"Yes, for a simple possession of a small amount of marijuana... When he was a juvenile. He was sixteen years old..."

"Well, this sentence is well within the guidelines, and if your client can maintain good behavior, he should have no problem making it out on his minimum..."

My attorney wanted to speak but was silenced by another stern glare. No matter how much of her heart was wrapped up in my case, she still had a family she was helping to provide for. The jurors seemed pleased with the verdict and the prosecution smirked malevolently at me. I looked back to see my mother, who was in tears. Then at my attorney as the weight of my sentence began to set in.

"Sorry," she whispered to me before dropping her head and then... I was alone. I realized there was nothing I could do and no one that would be able to help me. My sentence was in and I would be going to a state penitentiary for the next five years, at the least. I, too, said,

"Sorry," to my mother and she asked,

"Can I please hug him?" as I was being escorted out of the court room. I had done a good job of fighting back tears.

Since a child of four, I had always had to be strong for my mother, and this situation was no different. I've always been like that, no matter how heavy my load, I tried to carry the burden for others. I hate to see people hurting. So, although I was the one going away, I didn't want her to hurt any more than she had to.

In the back of the patty wagon, as I was being transported back to the County Prison, I cursed God vehemently. It was only then that I realized, I had been having one-way conversations with God my entire life - speaking to "something" that never responded - at least not audibly. My sentence was in and therefore there was no reason to ask for help now. So, I didn't. Instead, I retreated into the dark recesses of my mind.

...Flashback

It was the second marijuana stick and I was tired. It was a little after 11 p.m. and we still had a way to go to get to Jill's house in the suburbs of Central Pennsylvania.

"Nah, I'm ok, I'm good," I said as my girlfriend tried to pass the marijuana to me. At that point, I drifted off. Beneath my seat was a .45 caliber Ruger I had run from my county probation and was *"living on the lamb"* as they say. My source of income? A few pounds and a very loyal friend. Two weeks prior, I had walked into a pretty deadly situation. A group of guys from New York had positioned themselves on the same corner where my friends sold drugs – mainly cocaine, crack cocaine, and marijuana. This led to friction quickly and the friction inevitably boiled over to a full- fledged beef. I hadn't been a part of it because I was always out of town. However, you're often held accountable for the actions of those you associate with, so as soon as I was spotted with my friends, I was a target.

I had no idea shootouts had taken place as I had yet to be briefed on the war, but they had. So now, the turf battle was deadly. One day I was spotted by one of the Hispanic guys and in noticing I was affiliated with his enemy he pulled a tech-nine out on me. I was unarmed so I nodded my head to signal he had the power. I was at his mercy, but by the age of nineteen, I was already ready to die. He didn't shoot, but the threat was enough.

After he pulled off, I ran to my friend's house and told them what happened.

"Yo! What's goin' on over on thirteenth street? Dude just pulled out on me," I said slightly out of breath.

"What?! Man, we got beef with them n---------..." said one of my comrades. Another friend, Ronald, said nothing. He simply loaded a few slugs in his shotgun and had another comrade drive him over to the corner of Thirteenth and Chestnut Streets. Ten minutes later, he returned and smiled at me.

"I got him."

A few hours later, I learned he had shot the guy who pulled the tech-nine out on me, leaving the guy's arm slightly paralyzed. Because of this, I wanted to keep him beside me.

I brought him out of town with me and introduced him to my girl's friend. They hit it off, and now he was my muscle – although, I've never needed it – while I made my moves to keep myself alive while unable to get a job.

When I finally woke up – Ronald was asking us to stop the car. I didn't know exactly why and was too tired to find out. My girl asked me if it was ok and I said, "yes," not conscious enough to assess what he was doing.

We were in Downtown Carlisle; ironically enough right be- hind the courthouse. After a few minutes, I started to wonder what was taking him so long. After coming to, I had assumed he had only stepped out to urinate. But ten minutes was a long time so...

"I'll be right back," I said. The irritation clear in my tone and expression.

As always, I reached beneath the seat for my protection... It was gone. Immediately my awareness went up.

"He took the gun." I thought. Fear emerged as I realized he had run off to commit a robbery, a burglary, or both. My girlfriend shook her head at the same time I had. Ronald was loyal as a dog, but when it came to committing crimes or doing anything that took calculation, he was about as smart as one as well. I shut the door and quickly walked off to find him. He was only a few feet away. Right beneath the streetlight, in the middle of a downtown side street, he had four men at gun point. I quickly surveyed the scene. The guys looked young, very young - like teenagers. And they had no money.

"What the hell are you doing?" I asked. The boys looked scared, but for some reason relieved as they could see my appearance would mean the end of this terrifying event.

"Man, let's go!" I ordered and made my way back to the car. Just for the fun of it, he hit one of the kids in the head with the gun. Once I got back to the car, I was fully awake... and pissed!

"You ok?" my lady asked.

"Yeah, this dude is fuckin' robbing somebody," I said.

"What?!"

Before I could respond, Ronald jumped into the back seat.

"Let's go! Let's go!" he said.

I turned around as he went through his looted goods. A half-empty pack of cigarettes, two fugazy chains, and about two dol- lars and seventy-five cents. I just shook my head in disappointment as he discarded everything but the cigarettes.

...The Very Next Night

"Baby, baby, wake up! We're being pulled over."

For the second night in a row, I had fallen asleep on our way home. And for the second night in a row, I was being awaken to a situation I had to take immediate control of.

"For what? What happened? Were you speeding?" My first thought was she must've made a driving error. If so, we didn't have much to worry about. With panic in her tone, she exclaimed:

"No, nothing I swear to God."

I believed her. She never lied to me. It was the one thing I loved and respected about her. I glanced up in the rearview. Ronald was even more paranoid than she. His darker skin made the whites of his eyes that much more visible. They were lit up like miniature full moons.

"Yo... What are we going to do?!" He asked frantically. His eyes darted in every direction and he fidgeted like a terrified rodent. He kept looking back and his trepidation would prove to be calamitous.

"Nothing," I said. "We're going to pull over and see exactly why we're being pulled over."

The lights. There's something about the ominous nature of police sirens and lights. Even if you weren't guilty of any crime whatsoever, there was always a trembling trepidation attached to the sounds of sirens in your ears and the flash of lights in your rearview. I always charged it to the fact that those lights meant your freedom could be taken at any moment.

Ronald was way too jittery, and his actions were making me nervous. I knew immediately that something was wrong. This was no routine traffic stop. They had come with guns drawn. Jane rolled her window down and began to answer questions. By this time there was a police officer at my window as well. I kept my eyes forward and my hands visible.

"Why are you driving through here so late?" the officer asked. He was speaking to Jane, but his eyes were on everything but her - the make, model and color of the car, the interior of the car - the two passengers in the back seat. His partner's eyes were burning a hole in the side of my head.

"We were headed home," she answered honestly. From the corner of my eye, I could see Ronald making a move. He had noticed that his gun was slightly visible, so, foolhardily he reached down to shove it under Jane's seat.

"Put your fucking hands up!!!"

The officer who had been doing the questioning drew his weapon and pointed directly at Ronald.

This guy is going to get us all killed, I thought. And I quickly spat.

"Listen, my name is…. I do have a warrant. It's only probation. You can take me now!"

Luckily, he opened my door and began his pat down.

Eventually, we were all out of the car. Jane looked terrified and every time she was asked a question, she looked at me to see if she should respond, and if so, what she should say.

Eventually, we were taken downtown for more questioning. It seemed like it took them forever to get to me. I would eventually discover why. I had fallen asleep on the metal slab that served as a bed. Wrapped in my t-shirt, I laid in a fetal position to try to generate some heat. The lighting was dim and the walls cold and imposing. I quickly rehearsed my story, concocted my make-shift alibi, then drifted to sleep.

I'm not sure how long I was asleep, but the loud clanking of my steel door being opened awoke me and in a split second I recollected exactly where I was at.

"Let's go."

I followed the officer to another room for interrogation and to be honest, I was just happy to be out of that cold cell. The light in the room was brighter and it was a lot warmer.

"Where were you at last night?" the officer asked, after informing me the session would be recorded.

"With the mother of my daughter," I said quickly. The officers looked at each other with a glance that let me know - they knew I was lying.

"Are you sure?"

"Yeah," I shot back, less convincingly this time. I had even given them an address and phone number.

"Listen, your buddy already gave you up."

I paused. I figured this was a ploy to get me to tell on myself. However, recalling how afraid he had been, it wasn't inconceivable and something in my subconscious said They're telling the truth.

"I don't know what he told you, but..." They cut me off.

"Look."

They dropped his statement in front of me. It dropped like a feather; my heart dropped like a brick. Still skeptical, I searched for a sign the statement was forged. Maybe they were trying to trick me into confessing or informing. As I studied the handwriting, I knew it was his.

"We didn't mean to hurt anybody. We just wanted some money. We're sorry. We... We... We..."

I didn't say another word the entire time. This guy decided to do a crime and incriminated us all after being pressured. There was nothing else I could say. By the morning, we were being transported to the County Prison.

"I sure wish I could just use some southern law enforcement..." the arresting officer said as he led us to his car. I caught it, of course. I can't remember a time in my life when I wasn't conscious. I read **"The Destruction of The Black Civilization"** by Chancellor Williams by the age of eighteen, so I knew some simply have an innate hatred, disdain, and envy of the original man. His comment hadn't gone over my head. Like most things in life, it did fly completely over my co-defendant's'. What puzzled me, was why his brown partner ignored or pretended not to hear it. This man had basically said:

"I wish I could just lynch and hang you two niggers," and the Hispanic officer didn't even as much as cast a side-eye. I guess being the only melanated officer on the force, in a predominantly "white" town, left him feeling powerless. It's amazing how the fear of losing job security made slaves out of many men.

I looked the officer dead in his eyes, to let him know his remark hadn't gone unnoticed and that I completely comprehended the innuendo. In this instant however, I really had to "pick my battle". My hands were cuffed behind my back and it appeared his Hispanic partner would have overlooked any abuse I would have suffered at the hands of this man.

Once we were in our cells in the County Prison, I unleased my venom on my co-defendant.

"If you were going to admit and plead guilty – why would you say 'we'? I could've beaten this fuckin' case. You did that shit on your own!"

"I'm sorry..." Ronald said and tears began to pour down his face profusely. He tried to hug me, and I pushed him far away from me.

"Sorry won't get me out of here!" I snapped.

"I'm sorry I was scared. I didn't know... I didn't mean... I wasn't trying to get you into trouble... I don't know why I wrote 'we'; I was... I was nervous."

At that point, I realized I wasn't dealing with a rat, I was dealing with a terrified guy who thought "admission of guilt" would lessen the severity of his sentence... Now our sentence. Finally, I gave him a hug and told him, "It's cool. We'll get through this..."

He was relieved. Inside I was still pissed. However, I did have the preliminary hearing to look forward to. I hadn't robbed anyone. I appeared on the scene late and only stayed for a minute, maybe less.

"As long as the witness didn't I.D. me, I should be able to walk..." I reasoned.

Two months prior I would discover just how prevalent racism still was in America. Up until Jane, I had never officially dated a Caucasian woman. I had been intimate with one but was never bold enough to parade her as my woman. I still had a lot of spiritual growing to do. My life was spent - for the most part - in the slums of Harrisburg, PA where Europeans in impoverished neighborhoods was an oddity and interracial relationships were even more odd. Jane, however, had won my heart - not to mention - her home was far away from where I lived, which allowed me to sleep peacefully without the fear of being incarcerated by my probation officer, who had put out a warrant for my arrest.

Jane was from Perry County. The daughter of a well-to-do family. Her father drove trucks for a living and made enough to afford his wife the opportunity to be a "stay-at-home" wife. She had only chosen to continue working part time out of boredom – not necessity. They had a large house not too far from Musa Smith – a member of the only black family in Duncannon that I was aware of. According to Jane, Musa was a stand-out for Perry County Highschool who went on to play for the Georgia Bulldogs and then the Baltimore Ravens. I knew his story only because Jane told me – I think she had done so to make me comfortable.

Jane's father had the house built from the ground up and of all the things that amazed me – were the horses in the stable.

"You own horses?" I had asked in amazement. She didn't understand my shock. She also had never experienced poverty. They had a ton of land and a man-made path leading into the woods for dirt-bike and 4-wheeler riding. Equally impressive, was her father's rifle and shotgun collection he had decorated the ceiling with.

"You know if my dad were ever to catch you in here, he would try to kill you. He doesn't like black people." She had admitted. I pulled out my.45 and replied,

"Well, I would have to kill him if he didn't kill me first." I responded in all honesty and seriousness.

"What?! You're not going to kill my dad!" she had shot back angrily. It was a dose of reality and after we argued there was a slight disconnect. In silence, I pondered how I would have to then kill the entire family because if anyone lived to tell, the judges would not accept my self-defense pleas - I'd be going to prison forever. She must've come to her senses and understood that of course, in a life-or-death situation, I would have to protect myself. She nestled close to me to indicate she was sorry. I held her to show her it was okay.

"Don't worry, it'll never come to that." I said. We made love and all was forgotten.

I would soon discover that her mother smoked marijuana as well. She showed me the bowls her mother smoked.

"I'm going to get your mom high... forreal," I said one day as I finished rewrapping a Dutch Master cigar after filling it with Hydro.

"No," she said, but she too was smiling.

"Mrs. Suzy, You want to smoke with us?" I asked as Jane led me to her room. At first, she looked nervous, as if she had wanted to keep her marijuana use a secret. However, as I lit the tip of the Dutch Master, her curiosity got the best of her.

"What's that?" she asked.

"It's called a blunt. Here, take a pull..." I said, extending the cigar to her. She took a pull and before I could say "not too hard", she was coughing and choking. I was laughing, but Jane looked a little concerned.

"Take it easy, Mrs. Suzy, this ain't your bowl," I said smiling. After she recovered, she took a nice steady pull, and this time, her exhale was smooth.

"I like it," she said before passing it to Jane. We finished the stick and at first, I couldn't tell how she felt. She hopped up and began cleaning in a fast pace - a little too fast. Five minutes later, we looked into her room and she was out cold. Her head was hanging slightly off the bed and her feet dangled from the other end. Her glasses were crooked, and she was snoring. It was hilarious.

The next morning, we went outside to Jane's car. We were going to a tattoo shop in center-city; Jane planned to tattoo my initials on the arch of her foot. First, she stopped to check the mail. My face grew stern as I read the words "Nigger Lover" on her mailbox. Someone had vandalized her mailbox overnight. She was obviously upset, but more so concerned with how I was taking it.

I had learned stoicism at a young age so, besides a look of anger, just how agitated I was would remain a mystery to her.

"Are you ok?" she asked.

"Absolutely." I responded. And we pulled off.

The ride was spent in silence. We shared a marijuana stick and allowed the music to dictate the tone. I was quiet because of anger mixed with a slight amount of confusion. Jane's silence was predicated on feelings of guilt, empathy, and fear. Guilt: unfortunately, some people of European descent are forced to feel remorse for the near-sighted prejudices and racism of their people. Empathy: she could see that I was more hurt than anything. You don't know me personally, but you've lumped me into the "Nigger" box I had felt. And fear: she was fearful racism was going to jeopardize our relationship.

"You know you my baby..." I said, reassuring her after feeling the energy of her thoughts. She looked so relieved and gave me a huge hug.

Once downtown, Jane headed to the tattoo shop and I headed to a corner store for a box of cigars. The sun was at its zenith at this time; however, the heat was moderate. It was fall, so we weren't close enough to feel the intense heat. I glanced around at what was

"Downtown Duncannon".

It was more a retail corridor than a corporate district. There weren't many tall buildings, but the arrangement was nice and quaint.

After surveying the area, I reached down to tie my sneaker. Once I lifted my head and prepared to take a step, a muddy blue pickup truck roared past me.

"Haaaaaa! Get the fuck out of here!" the two men in the back shouted along with other profanities I couldn't make out. They flew past so quickly I had no time to react or respond. I just sat there looking dumb-founded. The only coherent thought was:

Those must be the guys who spray painted the derogatory epithet on Jane's mailbox.

Shaking off the shock, I continued on my mission, even quicker now, as the episode amplified my urge to smoke. I really needed to calm my nerves at this point.

As soon as I entered the store, I knew I shouldn't have. There were no signs saying, "Whites Only" or "No Coloreds Allowed", but there was definitely a pair of eyes saying it. The small mom and pop shop was rather bare so I had no intentions of venturing too far into the store. I did notice a cooler full of sodas, Gatorade, water and other liquid refreshments, which brought my forgotten thirst back to the forefront of my mind.

Through the reflection in the glass, I could see the clerks and their eyes were burning holes in my back. The husband sat tensely in a chair beside the counter and his wife waited impatiently for me to make a selection and quickly exit.

Finally, I settled on a bottled water and brought it to the counter.

"Can I have a pack of Dutch Masters please?" I asked.

I hadn't looked at the scarce tobacco shelf behind the woman - I had barely even looked at her. As I counted what I figured would be enough to cover the purchase, the round, brunette- haired woman said,

"We don't have none."

At that point I looked up and realized they had nothing but one pack of White Owls and two packs of Phillies.

"Ok, I'll take the Phillies." I said. I was slightly disappointed. Phillies had no natural leaf, just a paper wrapping that led to a harsh and distasteful smoking experience that would more than likely lead to lung problems in the future.

"We don't have none." She repeated, as if these were the only four words in her vocabulary. I looked at the woman questioningly and then at her husband who had inched up to the edge of his seat. I then looked at the packs of Phillies to ensure I was seeing correctly.

"The ones right behind you." I said looking puzzled. Maybe she wasn't sure exactly what I said.

"The Phillies..."

"I said we don't have none!" she reiterated. By this time, she had folded her arms against her breast and her husband was now so close to the edge of his seat that one move would have landed him on the floor. I was sure he had a pistol on him. Mine was in the car which did me no good. Not only was its location a problem, the fact that it wasn't registered was equally problematic.
I nodded my head and gave them both a side-eye before returning my water. There was no way I was going to buy anything from this store. Outside, I grabbed a bottle from the vending machine and before I could take a sip the blue pick-up returned. This time my anger was at its boiling point. I ran to the car as they laughed and screamed. As trash was thrown at me, I reached beneath the passenger seat. The truck was a little past me by this point, but I still aimed. I wanted so badly to fire but the realization of where I was kicked in immediately. The guys saw the gun and ducked. They sped off quickly and I ran into the tattoo shop.

"We gotta go!" I said anxiously.

"What's wrong? I'm not done yet," Jane responded. However, she could see the gumbo of emotions in my eyes. Luckily the tattoo shop owner did as well.

"This truck keeps riding by, I think it's the people that spray painted your mailbox. They're screaming 'Nigger' and tried to run me over. I just pulled out on 'em but I don't know who all saw."

Jane's eyes widened in fear. The tattoo artist's eyes reddened from anger.

"Fucking assholes! Here give me the gun!"

I was skeptical and reluctant to give him my weapon. What if he wanted to kill me, too? He sensed my apprehension and said,

"Listen, bro, not everybody thinks like those assholes. If someone did see, I don't want them to find your piece on you. I'm licensed and if anybody comes in here, I got the right to shoot 'em dead!" He was sin-cere - genuine - I could feel it. And I liked him. I also learned a valuable lesson. You can't judge an entire race for the ignorance of a few.

This guy was willing to hide me, cover for me, and kill for me if need be. I liked him.

"I'm just about done but that gives you guys enough time to let things cool down in case someone did see you... You won't look like you're running from the scene of a crime."

He was right. I gave him my firearm and took a seat - flipping through a tattoo magazine as he finished Jane's tattoo. Fifteen to twenty minutes later, she came back into the waiting area.

"You like?" she asked with a bright smile. It read "Baby SL." and had a detailed heart encompassing it. "I love it," I said, sure that my ego had added to my approval. She had just tattooed my name on herself to prove her love to me. "Pretty cool," the tattooist said. He was speaking on the love between two different races, not the artwork.

He returned my gun to me and I expressed my gratitude - for who he was as a man and individual. Two minutes later, Jane and I were on our way back to her house. It was time to make love.

A few weeks into our relationship and I had decided to bring Rue out to meet

Jane's friend. They didn't mesh immediately but soon Jill took a liking to him. We had a good time in those few weeks leading up to the arrest. Jill's family had plenty money as well and we had a ball, riding four-wheelers along the trails in the wooded areas surrounding her house. Every day was a party it seemed. There was never a shortage of THC and the spirits flowed like a perpetual fountain courtesy of Jill's family liquor storage. I wasn't much of a wine drinker, but the bourbon, cognac, and whiskey were all fine with me.

When it comes to character, there are always small warnings that signal larger defects. Ronald began to make to make minor mistakes that led me to believe not only was he not very strategic, but that he may not be able to hold water. The tongue is very light, yet few people can hold it.

The morning on the day of our arrest, Ronald thought it was a good idea to dump the ashtray, and trash on the road right outside of Jill's highway. Her neighbor – who also happened to be her aunt – saw it and made a comment. We all commented on how dumb it was and, because of his ego, him and I fought. He mentioned something about not speaking to him like that – which I immediately translated to:

"You hurt my feelings and made me look and feel inferior in front of women".

Embarrassed, he approached me aggressively. One thing I never do is wait to be swung on first, so I clocked him square in his eye. He staggered back, then came forward with even more rage.

I swung a nice two piece, both blows landed, but he was close enough to grab me. Ronald had been a pretty good wrestler on the high school team, and before I knew it, my feet were off the ground and my head was headed towards it. Luckily my head tucked in time, and my shoulders and upper back took the brute of the impact. After squirming my way out of his clutches, we stood up and, again, I threw my hands. I was more a boxer than a brawler, as my slight 5'8, 145-pound frame dictated this defense mechanism.

Two lightning quick jabs and a right hook, and I had Ronald slightly dazed. It was at this point I looked into his eyes and saw pain. I immediately dropped my hands. Still in the heat of the moment - it was hard to embrace and forgive - but there was a subtle exchange of remorseful energy through eye contact.

In silence, we headed towards Harrisburg to re-up and that night, we made the trip through Carlisle that would ultimately lead to my demise and subsequent rebirth.

At the preliminary, I was still sure I would be vindicated. I mean, I was innocent - why wouldn't I be? The preliminary trial is held to see if there's enough evidence to bound the case over for court. Considering I hadn't done anything that night, I was sure justice would be served and I would be set free. Ronald had plead guilty and that was on him. I hadn't because I wasn't, so I was actually happy this day had finally arrived. I was really about to experience a rude awakening as far as the legal system was concerned.
Ronald and I were led to seats in the last row of a fairly small courtroom - the seats across were vacant and then - there was Jane. She looked nervous. I knew they had already begun to tempt her with deals to fold on Ronald, but by the way she looked at me, I could see I must have been included in the indictment. Still, we smiled at each other through the pain. We loved each other.

After Jane, Jane's mother came in. She seemed to be more un- der-standing. As easy as it would have been to view me as the rea- son she was in this mess, she knew her daughter's choices had led her to this point. She knew the real me. She could see my early decision-making was a re-action to poverty and the habits of the impoverished.

Jane's father, however, had killed me, resurrected me, and killed me again with his stare. His nostrils flared and his eyes were reddened by the inferno within as he now had to protect his daughter because of her affinity for an African American misfit and his Black hoodlum friend. I just couldn't match his stare. Not because of fear, but because I, too, had a daughter.

Although four victims had been involved in the case, only one was called to testify. I figured that would be in my favor. Once he testified, I was even more convinced I'd be vindicated.

"Do you recognize the defendant?" the prosecutor asked in reference to Ronald.

"Yeah, that's the guy that robbed us. That's the guy that hit me in the head with the gun."

Just hearing him repeat the story had pissed me off. The night of the robbery - the quick glance I had taken at the victims had led me to believe they were all teenagers but seeing them in court and then reading the paperwork had confirmed it. The guy testifying was only 18. The oldest was 19 and another was 17. The fourth was unknown because he didn't want to testify. He made a statement but wanted nothing to do with the court proceedings.

Ronald had dropped his head in shame. I believe the weight of the case and sheer gravity had something to do with the lowering of his head as well, not to mention his inability to look the witness in his eyes.

The same question was asked of me.

"Do you recognize the defendant?"

His eyes scanned me, and, without the slightest hesitation, he said,

"No!"

The judge and prosecutor both looked shocked. My public defender looked as happy as one could while feigning stoicism. I smiled. Jane smiled as well.

"Are you sure?" the D.A. asked again in an insinuative manner. Once again, he looked at me, but even more briefly. The second look was not to make sure he wasn't mistaken, but because he had been asked rhetorically. Even more emphatically, this time he said:

"No, I've never seen him before in my life!"

That was it. I should have walked out of that courtroom a free man. That was actually the snowball's chance my P.D. and I had discussed.

If the witness couldn't ID me, the prosecution had no case against me. What heightened my joy, was the fact that my attorney now believed me and realized I had been telling her the truth! I hadn't stayed out of the car long enough for anyone to identify me. I hadn't robbed anyone that warm, summer night, June 12, 2002. This time she allowed her smile to show. She and my mother had already begun to form a little bond: she being a mother herself. She must've known or been able to imagine how it would have felt to hear her son swear he was innocent, but to not be believed and potentially prosecuted because of this disbelief.

The D.A., however, wasn't satisfied. He was determined to convict me as well as Ronald. A crime against four whites had been committed by two black males in a predominately white town. There was no way in Hell he was letting me out of this. He pulled out a piece of paper, preparing to hand it to the judge. At first, I had no idea what it was, but then he asked:

"I'll ask you again, are you sure no one else was at the scene? I have a statement from the co-defendant indicating he had not committed this crime alone and that the defendant had worked as an accomplice..."

"Hand me the statement," the judge asked the D.A. after the victim then stated:

"Well, if you say he was there, then I guess so. I don't remember seeing him."

My attorney looked defeated. I just shook my head, then dropped it, staring at the papers and files on the desk in front of me. I knew it was over. Ronald's incriminating statement had buried me along with the prosecutor's determination to secure another conviction for the state.

The rest of the trial was a nebulous ocular blur, and monotonous mumble. The only thing I heard clearly was my order to stand up and follow the officers out of the courtroom.

As we headed back to the prison, my spirit was suffering from an inner conflict, as ominous as the future appeared, I realized I still had a fighting chance. I still had a trial coming in which I could further defend myself and prove my innocence. Ronald was more than willing to write a new statement, one in which he would clarify his statements and claim full responsibility for the crime.

A spiritual battle was also in the making. As a child, Christianity as a religion and way of life just made no sense and didn't fit into the fabric of my spiritual makeup. My affinity for Jesus, however, was unwavering...

"I love Jesus," I told my cellmate.

"It's Christianity that makes no sense to me. Over and over, Jesus is telling me to give glory to God, that he's helpless without the Father, yet I'm always being told to praise Jesus' name. To give him glory. When we pray at home, we always end with "in Jesus' name...""

"Have you ever read the Quran?" my cellmate asked. I hadn't.

"Well - no." I had heard of it but had never given it much thought. I knew as a child, before my mother accepted Jesus as her *"Lord and Savior"*, that she would instruct me to say: *"Wa Laykum as Salaam"* to the few strangers who had greeted us with *"As'Salaamu Alaykum"*.

"You should. It'll clear your confusion..."

And so, I began to read the Quranic narrative of Jesus Christ, or as he was referred to in the Quran, Isa Ibn Maryam *"Jesus, The Son of Mary"*.

The truth can be startling initially, especially if it challenges every-thing you've ever believed. I experienced this fear to "switch faiths". I im-mediately said a prayer:

"Please, God, help me learn this truth, but never lose my faith in Jesus."

As soon as my prayer ended, I heard a man talking in mathematical and scientific terms about Jesus. His speech culminated with:

"...And if he said the same power is in you, what is this saying?"

The crowd looked dumbfounded.

"He's saying the power of God is in you. You're God." He quoted Psalms 82:6 and corroborated with John 10:34-35. I immediately leafed through my Bible to the passages he quoted. I was astounded. Why had I never read this? Or why had my mind been programmed to read over these verses without a second thought? Why had no preacher ever read these in church? I immediately approached the man who had introduced himself as *King*.

"I want to learn," I said. I was unsure of exactly what to say.

"Learn what?" he questioned, though the look in his eyes let me know he knew exactly what I meant.

"How to talk like that," I said naively. He smiled at my innocence, but I could see he was proud of my courage. It takes a lot for a man to admit to another man that he would like to be taught, it's an admission of inferiority on some level but a sign of superiority to the wise.

"It's not how you talk it's how you live. Mathematics is to be applied in your ways and actions, not just your words." he said.

"I know... But in order to live properly, I feel I need to learn what you teach."

And that began my introduction to the "Nation of Gods and Earths", or the "Five-Percenters".

King gave me the lessons one sentence at a time. Each sentence would become a Degree I had to log to memory in order to be able to recite them verbatim. As was custom, I chose an attribute. Typically, one would choose a name from "The Supreme Alphabet", or simply an enlightening word describing attributes of God. I chose "Infinite - Infinite God Allah". Your last name would be Allah because you were now coming into the realization that you were indeed a manifestation of God's creative will, or Allah "Arm, leg, leg, arm, head" as my brothers loved to articulate it.

My loyal heart kept me devoted to the teachings of "The Father", and his successors and I logged the 120 Degree Lessons to memory and began using them to guide others to spiritual freedom and mental emancipation.

Eventually, I would learn that the man we so affectionately referred to as "The Father" - a term I appreciated as I had

had no fatherly guidance and these lessons were guiding me to manhood - was a man named Clarence Smith. He would later be referred to as Clarence 13x after the denouncing of his branding - the slave-name that had been given to his ancestors. Clarence 13x had split from the Nation of Islam and started his own group. The Nation of Gods and Earths.

The issue I was having was, to fulfill my prayer, and "know" God intimately, I had to trace all teachings to their original source.

After realizing Christianity was a man-made religion, my pursuit was of that which was God-sent, not man-made. I had to trace Clarence's teachings to their source. That source - I would find - was the Nation of Islam.

My issue then with the NGE was the same I would later have with the NOI. If you're stating you're not part of something, why take its core teachings and not created your own lessons, words, terminology, rituals and customs? I would eventually learn that the Nation of Islam is all wise and does everything right and exact and I just had a very immature, indoctrinated understanding of what

Islam was. It wasn't my religion; it was my nature and therefore my way of life.

Then there was the myopic view of theology and the Supreme Being. I knew the term "Muslim" meant "one who is in submission to Allah." So how could one be a Muslim and Allah at the same time? Because of these and other glaring discrepancies, a few of the brothers decided it was time to "rewrite our history" or - reword the lessons. This meant the lessons were imperfect - which is very *hue*man. I, however, was seeking God's perfection. As stated, these were "my" issues as I would eventually discover the wisdom that reconciled the faults of all man-made attempts to name the nameless.

Eventually, the linguistic aerobics, battles of the mind, and "talk" wore on my spirit. I didn't want to wake up and discuss "Today's math" just so we could see who had the sharpest "sword" or tongue. I wasn't here for petty ego battles. I wanted to understand the Creator I revered and help change the course of "my people". Period. I wasn't here to waste time or play games.

Eventually, I would come to understand it was more so a philosophical system built around the espousal of the best parts of the world's many religions, schools of thought, and walks of life to create a "new way of life." In essence it was a shiny new key to open that same ancient door.

I remember having a debate with a brother about the word "Allah". I kept explaining its Arabic roots and meanings, how it was one of the oldest names for the (Al) Deity (Lah). In Aramaic and Hebrew, it was "El", "Elah", or "Elohim". The E was simply replaced by the Alif in Arabic. He debated it meant "Arm, Leg, Leg, Arm, Head". He simply couldn't separate the acronym from the true definition. He was indoctrinated. That which was meant to free the mind simply exonerated him from the prison of religion and incarcerated him in a philosophical penitentiary. Eventually, my mind felt overfed, but my heart and soul felt malnourished. My spirit still had some ascending to do.

The surpassing of the Nation of Gods and Earths to attain full-awakening and higher consciousness would not happen for some years, however. For now, at the tender age of twenty - it was a god-send - literally. I looked at King like a father. I knew he was flawed - but that didn't mat-ter. I admired the man. Together, we revolutionized my diet as I eradicated pork, then beef, then chicken, and finally meats altogether from my diet.

I mastered my Degrees in record speeds. My confidence was swelling. I no longer felt bad for dropping out of high school because the knowledge I had now was far superior to that contained withing the rigid framework of public-school curriculum. A curriculum that had more to do with indoctrination than edification.

As Karl Evanzz stated in his book "The Judas Factor" in regards to the Honorable Elijah Muhammad:

"Although Muhammad's formal education had ended in the fourth grade, Fard (Muhammad) gave him a list of one hundred and six books, including the Bible and the Quran, which provided him with knowledge of things that even the graduates of Ivy League schools know little about."

I began teaching my family "knowledge of self" and anyone around me that would listen.

King taught me properly. He did not allow me to see the entire body of lessons. I was only awarded with the next Degree once I memorized, comprehended, and could recite the Degree in front of me. I could not learn who the "Colored man" was until I mastered the science and understanding of who the "Original man" was. Who was he? "The Original Asiatic Black man of Asia, The Maker, The Owner, The Cream of planet Earth: The Father of civilization and God of the Universe."

I had always been a precocious child. In my teens, I was wise beyond my years, and now, approaching Twenty-One, my wisdom was increasing and I was surpassing my peers. This is not any compliment to me, but an ode to true knowledge, wisdom, and understanding.

Ronald and I had put his blunder behind us and were now back on good terms. I think we both knew things would never be the same, but we needed each other in this place to a degree, and I just didn't have it in me to expose his mistake. He wasn't an informant, nor was he a stool pigeon. He was simply a terrified man who accidentally implicated me in his crime. He apologized so much I asked him to stop.

The D.A. really had no plans of letting me get out of this. They were convinced I was just as guilty as Ronald, and so after offering me a 4 ½ -9 to take a plea deal, the lowest they would ever go was a 4-8. 5-10 years was the maximum sentence I was looking at, so it would have been foolish to take any deal. I would simply take the case to trial and continue to defend my innocence.

Shortly after meeting King, I did meet a Muslim brother from Philadelphia. I noticed how he shunned the teachings of the Five-Percenters, but never in an arrogant or confrontational manner. I believe he realized that King was firmer in his convictions than I, so one day he asked me to attend Jumu'ah. I told him I would.

That Friday, I walked the corridor towards the chapel. The Chaplain's office area had been transformed into a serene scene I could only describe as "Middle-Eastern" at the time. My senses were immediately overwhelmed by the aesthetically pleasing, and spiritually alluring ambiance of the room.

Beautiful carpets with amazingly intricate designs were spread out on the floor. The scent of incense permeated the "mosque". I could smell fragrant oils rising from the skins of the 6 or 7 men in the area. There were mystic looking Qurans with Arabic writing that, at the time, I could not make out.

I scanned the room for the humble soul that had invited me to this gathering, but he hadn't shown up yet. The men did cast suspicious glares at me, which I understood. I had yet to introduce myself or join in on the rituals they were partaking in methodical ablutions and peculiar standing, bowing, and prostrating movements. I prayed he'd come soon to ease the "suspicion" and immediately after my silent supplication, he did.

"Ahhh, you made it, brother. I didn't think you'd come,": he said joyfully. His eyes smiled wider than his mouth did, and his hand-shake morphed into a loving, brotherly embrace.

"I said I would," was all I could come up with as I smiled back. "Ok, so just observe. Just listen and observe. If you don't like it, you never have to come again. If you do, and in shaa Allah you will, then you will come again every or any Friday you want."

"Ok," I said. And he went to greet his brothers. He must've explained to his brothers the reason for my presence because they too smiled invitingly.

My father was Muslim, and I had been born into a Muslim family but after my father and mother split my mother would slowly break away from Islam. The only thing I remembered from our short-lived time in the Deen of Islam was the greeting:

"As 'Salaam Alaikum."

"Wa Laikum As 'Salaam."

After the leader said a short speech, a large portion of which was in Arabic, the men lined up for prayer. It was one of the most ambient, moving moments of my life. The recitation of the Quran was more beautiful than any song I had ever heard. The unison which the brothers moved during prayer was simply amazing. I left that day in a state of spiritual euphoria I had never experienced in my life - and I hadn't even partaken in it.

The brother who invited me could see it in my eyes and he smiled again.

"How did it feel?" he asked.

"That was amazing, brother," I said.

"Well, like I said, we're here every Friday, so in shaa Allah we see you again."

"You will..." I responded. He shook my hand and made his way to his cell block as I made my way towards mine.

When I made my way into the cell block, I spotted King and, for some reason, I felt shame. I felt almost as if I had betrayed him somehow. I knew that what he was teaching me completely contradicted what I had just sat through. We didn't pray because we didn't believe in a spook god. I was sure he would be disappointed if he found out I had just sat through Jumu'ah and, not only sat through it, but thoroughly enjoyed it. My plan was to not mention it, and quickly wipe the euphoric look from my face. That plan was quickly thwarted, however.

"Peace, God," he saluted. "Peace to the God," I returned.

"Where'd you go?" he asked. It was a genuine question. He truly had no idea, and if it wasn't for a visit or some type of program, it wasn't normal for inmates to be gone from the block too long. As much as I wanted to, I couldn't lie to him. I admired the man too much to allow dishonesty to potentially ruin our relationship. It was at that very moment I would learn just how wise King really was.

"Jumu'ah," I said. It was almost as if I expected a scolding, the way I admitted it. I searched his eyes for disappointment. There was none. Instead, amazement - even happiness - seemed to brighten his countenance. He chuckled...

"Ok, Young God..." he said, almost proudly. "Did you like it?"

My eyes lit up in amazement and relief.

"I did. It was... It was peaceful, God. Like, it really spoke to my spirit."

He nodded as if he knew the feeling, the feeling that was now returning to my heart as the wall of shame came tumbling down.

"That's the believers, right there... I'm glad you got to experience that..." he said, smiling. We walked back to my cell and I detailed my experience. Afterwards, I asked for my next Degree, however. I was still very loyal to him and the lessons he was teaching me. I still had to finish that school of thought, but my experience in Jumu'ah at the County Prison would never be forgotten.

Eventually, I would have my trial where I was convicted as an accomplice to a robbery. Apparently "accomplice liability" carried just as much weight as actually committing the crime. I was subject to, and eventually sentenced to, the same 5-10-year term as Ronald. Jane and Jill both received 4 years of probation - no jail time - for the same accomplice liability I was. By that time, I was too exhausted to even feel a way about it. My mother cried, Ellen, my public defender, apologized and, subsequently, retired after no longer having the heart to fight and witness such injustices. I just stared into the soulless, blue eyes of the judge I now viewed as a devil, and said bluntly, "No," when asked if I had any- thing to say. You can't appeal to the heart of a heartless creature, and thanks to King's lessons and my experience, I realized this courtroom was full of them. The District Attorney had pushed for twenty years to be added to the tail end of my sentence - to keep me in the system even longer. The judge deliberated but ruled against it.

He ran some scripted speech about how he was sparing me and that this would be a chance to better myself. I was 21, I looked young, but I wasn't as naïve as he thought. I understood the Prison Industrial Com-plex as well as the psychological ramifications of being

incarcerated. I understood I'd wear that felony like a badge of dishonor for nearly the rest of my life. I understood prison was dangerous and I could die inside. I wanted to laugh, but I remained stoic. I kissed my mother, told her I love her, and apologized.
"I'm sorry, Mom... I'm sorry for disappointing you..."

"I love you, son, don't be sorry... You be strong. You'll get through this."

For her I smiled. Then shut a major portion of my body down to prepare for 5-10 years of imprisonment... my heart.

I began to get into fight after fight and confrontation after confrontation. I didn't care about anything anymore. I would miss the most precious years of my daughter's life. Jane and other female pen pals faded to black after hearing how long I'd be away. I kept learning the lessons of the Five-Percenters and really could believe there were human devils in existence now. God, Allah, whatever people called the Deity, most certainly appeared to be a "spook" now. What kind of loving, compassionate god would let this happen to an innocent man? I pondered. I was bitter inside. Jane had told me her father threw all my belongings into a pile on her lawn with a picture of me on top and burned it, like some sort of Ku Klux Klan ritual. Devil! I thought when she said it. I remember going out on a visit to see my mother with blood still running from a scar on my face from a fight that end- ed less than ten minutes before she arrived.

"What's going on, baby?" she asked.

"Nothing. Some dude disrespected me, so we got into it. Don't worry, he looks worse than me."

She looked worried. Meanwhile, a guy in a booth four for five seats down was arguing with his woman. They were so loud I could barely hear.

"Yo! Can y'all keep it down, fam?!" I said.

"What, bruh? Mind ya fuckin' business," he shot back. "What?!" I jumped up to attack him as well.

"Sit down please!" I respected my mom's wishes but promised him I'd see him later.

Two weeks later there was a loudmouth guy from New York. I beat him so bad he began to bite me. I still have the scar to this day. It's not that I felt unbeatable, it's that I didn't care if I died. I had nothing left to live for. I had thrown my future away. I knew exactly how society would now view me. I could see I was disappointing King, but also knew he understood. He had his own problems, however. He was sentenced to twenty years in the Federal system. I lost my guide as well as my God in a two-month span. Luckily, I was transferred to the Camp Hill State Penitentiary not too much longer after.

Without King, I felt slightly lost. I had pretty much mastered my lessons, but he had given me the rest to learn on my own. I did begin to teach a few of the guys I knew from around the way. Blissful nostalgia of my visit to Jumu'ah would arise periodically, and I did try to converse with a group of Muslims at one point while in Camp Hill Prison. It was very unfruitful.

Twice I had run into Muslims of the pure faith - Orthodox Sunni Muslims - if you would. At the time, neither had compelling enough invitations to get me to revert. In prison, because people join for all the wrong reasons - superficial reasons - like protection, acceptance, and heritage, Muslims just resembled another gang. I was seeking "wahjullah" the face of Allah. I was seeking a return to my natural, spiritual disposition - fitra - as it is referred to in Arabic. Also, because of the simplicity of the religion I suppose, most of the Muslims I had run into were incapable of establishing their "proofs" as eloquently as the Five-Percenters had. No matter how truthful or false, elocution is a very persuasive tool. I would later read a saying of the prophet Muhammad indicating how hypnotic words can be. "Be careful, for there is much magic in eloquence."

In the County, the brother who had given me the Quran to read as a means of clarifying my curiosity about the true nature of Jesus, had no "words" of his own, nor did his actions reflect the ways of a man in submission to Allah. He had simply given me Al-kitab'ul Allah and left me to figure its meaning on my own. Even that was enough, however, to start me on the path.

The aim of the Quran is to initiate and bring to fruition an intellectual revolution within man. The expression used by the Quran for this is "Ma'arifah" - Realization of Truth.

"And when they listen to the revelation
   received by the Messenger, thou wilt
  see their eyes overflowing with tears,

> for they recognize the truth: They
> pray: "Our Lord! We believe; write us
> down among the witnesses."
> —5:38

Unfortunately, I would have to come to this realization later - a lot later. Because of my time with King, I learned to never take anything on face value, to be able to show and prove and to make sure the knowledge being proposed to me was actual fact. So, as I sat in the mess hall with a group of Believers from Philadelphia, I carried these same sentiments. They spoke more from a memorized, indoctrinated standpoint, and before I simply accepted what they said, I asked for proofs. The proofs weren't scientific or mathematical in nature — simply Hadiths (sayings and actions) of the prophet that were collected almost a century after he passed. When I gave my understanding, or Tafseer, of a Quranic ayat, I was told there were Tafseer written by Ibn Katheer and a few other renowned scholars from which I should derive my understanding. Basically, he was telling me I couldn't think for myself; he actually said words very close to that. I just couldn't accept that - at all. I know I was given an intellect and individual soul for a reason. Yet, he was telling me to suppress them and blindly follow other men's conclusions —

robotically. My soul has always loved spirituality, but I vehemently reject indoctrination. To a degree, I am still this way to this day.

I quickly broke away from them and sought out a few Five-Percenters. And for the duration of my incarceration that's who I associated with – up until the very end of my imprisonment.

Being as though Camp Hill was just a classification jail, my stay there was short. After about a month, I was packing my belongings and heading to my "home" jail. Sci-Albion.

Like an animal being led to a zoo for economic purposes, my hands and feet were cuffed in shackles as we made our way to the State Penitentiary of Albion, Pennsylvania. Physically, we weaved through a maze of country roads, mentally I weaved through the maze of the prison industrial complex.
Although my stay at Albion – "Far Beyond" as it was referred to – was short, the seeds of my revolution would be planted almost immediately.

I met a man named General. A Rastafarian originally from Jamaica, via New York he had been incarcerated for a major amount of marijuana amongst other charges. He took a liking to me rather quickly. I've always been a sponge and I've never had a problem putting myself under the tutelage of one willing to teach.

General was a slim built, dark-skinned man whose locks hung to the back of his calves. He kept them neatly wrapped in what appeared to be a Turban of knotted hair he called his "crown". General was a vegan and I, too, soon became one. To this day I miss our circuits around the track in the prison's yard, where he'd pass me invaluable pearls of wisdom – free of charge. Not only did he revolutionize my diet – he taught me the game of chess (I should say increased my technique and patience in it as I had long before learned the movement of the pieces) and, most importantly, he helped me forgive my father.

Up until meeting him, I blamed my gather for my plight in life – something I had learned from my mother.

I still remember his words. As we prepared for a game of chess, and he wrapped and neatly placed his crown upon his head, I vented my frustrations for my father's absence and lack of guidance and support. After hearing enough of me berating my father he said:

"Listen, Young Lion, I know you love your mother, but her side is all you've heard." Delicately - trying to avoid hurting my feelings - he said,

"She may be just as in the wrong, Bredren. You, - Young Star - be patient - one day you may meet your father and realize your mom was equally to blame." He stopped there, made brief eye contact to ensure I under- stood, then unrolled the chess board. He didn't say another word nor did I.

A veil had just been lifted, but now I was even more confused. The clouds of confusion dissipated quickly as I realized he was right. All I knew of my father was what my mother had told me. He had never been able to tell me his side. The few minutes I did have with him - when we some-how were able to hunt him down for child support purposes - he had told me, of course, he loved me. Had my mother also played a part in me not having a father? The question haunted me until I had children of my own. Of course, she had played a part in it, I would later come to realize - as much as I loved her, I could not ignore the fact that she was indeed a mortal woman,

riddled with flaws and capable of mistakes.
It was the role of the overseers to divide the family unit. This starts with making the woman rebellious. Of course, my father was to blame as well. But now I had to admit to myself that Umi could and should share in the blame of the breaking of the family unit as well. I love her immensely no matter what – Shaitan is an avid enemy to man as well as emotion that overrides logic – she's forgiven – both of my parents are.

Leaving General was hard. I must admit, at twenty-one, I was still seeking a true father figure. Not the spineless addicts that had filtered in and out of my mother's life – a real man with wisdom. From King to General, both had – in some way – temporarily filled the void created by my father's absence.

Albion was cold – to say the least. Erie was bordered by Buffalo, NY and Canada and this location had brought with it the same gusty winds and heavy snowfall as its bordering cities. I remember seeing snowfall in May at one point. The climate wasn't the worst part, however – the distance from home was. At a five- hour driving distance, there was no way

I'd receive a visit, nor did I want or expect anyone I loved to drive that far. A brother, who I now realize was a Fruit of Islam, had given me an essay written by Mutula Shakur. He was speaking about the psychological ramifications of prison and how the prison industrial complex was a capitalistic business like any other business. The prisons were owned and operated by private business owners who profited from housing the bodies of inmates. This explained why even those convicted of petty crimes, like drug possessions - which warranted drug rehabs - not prison - were sent to these modern-day plantations.

Obviously, the part that stuck out the most for me was how he stated that the shipping of men so far from their homes was intentional and not accidental. This was to further the divide in families, making it increasingly hard for inmates to receive visits, which would provide the emotional support to maintain sanity. Out of sight, out of mind was a cliché you hear very often in prison and the further out of sight you were, the further out of minds you'd be.

Another monumental figure in the reshaping and remolding of my mind was T. Williams. He was from the same city as I, so it was a lot easier to make a connection. He gave me the encouragement to take my book-writing seriously and the advice to see it as the business venture it was.

He, too, had knowledge of self and I felt and still do feel - he was brilliant - a genius even. He had given me many books on Dr. Malachi York, a man I had never heard of up until this point. Not only did he give me the books, he patiently explained them to me. He was probably the closest to a "king-like" figure I would ever get to again. His diet wasn't as rigid as the General's, as he catered to a protein-based diet geared to build muscle and expedite "healthy" weight gain. He drank a lot of protein shakes - raw eggs, bananas, milk, nutmeg and cinnamon and worked out religiously. I inherited his love for exercise.

At the same time, he had a lot on his mind and I always sensed a heavy weight on his soul. I learned over time to respect his space. Not too many monumental things happened at Albion. I did meet two brothers from the Moorish Science Temple established by Noble Drew Ali. I was given a Circle-Seven Koran from which I drew a lot of wisdom as well. I did wonder why these figures had been hidden from me. Cheik Ante Diop, Ivan Van

Sertima, Noble Drew Ali, Malachi York, Anthony T. Browder, Dr. Henry Clark, Naim Akbar - and a host of other great black authors, doctors, and researchers were revealed to me during my stay at Albion, which lasted two years.

I still can't remember why, but after those two years, I was transferred to Sci-Fayette, a maximum-security prison that ranked high on the "most notorious" list. Why they were shipping me there makes no sense unless you know the nature of the beast - then nothing he does surprises you.

From the very first glance at the façade of Sci-Fayette, my spirit was de-pressed. The grass was dry and patchy whereas the grass at Sci-Albion was a lot more lush, green, and neatly manicured. The buildings were dirty and dungeon-like in appearance while, on the contrary, those at Albion appeared to be new- er, or newly renovated. The gates creaked, the guards were disrespectful, the barbed wire was imposing, and the ambiance was disheartening.

"This jail is a shit hole," one inmate said, as we sat, shackled and chain on the tightly packed bus.

"It's a maximum-security jail... It's full of lifers and long-timers." an-other added.

"My man said they just got off lock down 'cause some guy got stabbed a third interjected.

I just listened and each comment heightened my apprehension. I wasn't necessarily scared, however, just preparing myself for what was sounding like the harshest of my prison experiences thus far. My assumptions proved to be true.

The first day I was let out for yard I would experience the type of rebellions that would fashion my thoughts for the rest of my life.

Ominous gray clouds littered the sky like dirty cotton balls. They were stacked so the blue appearance of the abode was hidden. A storm was approaching, but that wasn't enough to stop me, or the majority of the inmates in this camp, from going out to enjoy the fresh air. Initially, nothing appeared to be out of the ordinary. I ran into a familiar face from the neighborhood and we basked in the momentary nostalgia of memories. I also saw a group of men "building". For some reason, maybe the antenna-like nature of the pineal gland, I knew they were members of the Nation of Gods immediately.

One threw me a peace sign and I returned the gesture. The "Peace Sign" of the Five-Percenters was no ordinary spreading of the two fingers, however. As King had explained, there can be no division if we are to attain peace. So, the index and middle fingers are always held tight together, and the hand is held over the heart. I excused myself to greet my brothers.

"Peace, God!" A dark man with glasses said.

"Peace, God!" I returned.

"What's your attribute?" he asked after we finished our embrace.

"Infinite God Allah!" I responded proudly.

"And yours?"

"Wise Intellect Allah," he said.

"Where you from?" he asked. I told him my physical manifested in Harrisburg, but my mind's origin was the universe.

"I'm from Pittsburgh," he had responded. I told him I want- ed to finish talking to my comrades, but that we would build later. Indeed, we would. Little did I know Wise was a kindred spirit and we were in very similar spaces in our spiritual development. As the recreational yard period ended, I walked towards the gate but was stopped by a militant brother who was a member of the Nation of Islam.

"Hold on, young Brother!" he said, using his arm as a bar to stop me from leaving. I looked him in his eyes to sense a sign of threat. There was none.

"What's going on?" I asked.

"We striking. Nobody's going back in. They refuse to give the men cigarettes, proper access to the law library, and other liberties."

He was serious. His face shown conviction and his eyes gave no hint of compromise. I simply said,

"Ok!" and stood beside him as the first of many rebellious strikes began. Strangely, I had no fear, even after the guards threatened us with violence. And the guard in the watch tower loaded rubber bullets into his shotgun. My blood was boiling. I didn't even smoke cigarettes, but if it was a right due to the men, I was down for the cause. Inmates and guards exchanged threatening stares as tensions rose rapidly.

We stayed out for almost two hours and, eventually, we won – we were accommodated. That very day I realized just how powerful unity and courage were. To this day, it's the very reason why I can't understand why, or relate, to people who don't, or won't, stand up for themselves – for their rights.

Another instance was a hunger strike we started. The serving sizes and the option for healthy alternatives were insufficient. So, for three days no one went to the mess hall when chow was called. The couple who did, looked weak and knew they did. Again, it was a beautiful struggle for freedom, justice, and equality. And the unity and camaraderie it spawned was awe-inspiring. The men who were considered indigent and had little to no support, were provided for by those who were. We shared food and we shared knowledge. We ridiculed and ostracized the ones too weak to join the resistance, and for months after, peace permeated the penitentiary. White, Black, Hispanic, it didn't matter, in that moment in time, we had become brothers. I will never forget that feeling so long as I live.

A year or so into my stay, a few brothers decided to start our own group. The prison had anger management classes, drug and alcohol classes, etc. But we were ready to take back our communities and it would start right here, in SCI-Fayette.

Along with a wonderful, beautiful, amazing female counselor, we started "The Men's Growth Group" (MGG). Every week we would get together so "each one could teach one, according to his knowledge".

All were invited. Christians, Hebrew Israelites, Moors, Muslims, Five-Percenters, Nation of Islam members, Asafo (African Warriors), Latin Kings, Agnostics - no matter the banner you came under - if you promoted unity to combat the divide and conquer strategies that had decimated poor neighborhoods and poor families - you were invited.

For the most part, the aim of the group was achieved, and I would consider it a success. Brother James made us aware of the U.C.C. Act, maritime laws and gaining sovereignty over the birth names and social security numbers that had been "corporatized" unbeknownst to the recipient of said names and numbers. Brother Melchizedek informed us of how important the Nation of Islam was to our physical and spiritual rebirth. Brother Piper awoke our ancestral connection to our ancestors and the motherland. We read poetry, news articles, and anything that would spark the flame of rebellion and awakening. Once the Million Man March came, we raised enough money to send twenty-one children to the event. I was amazed at the mobilization of potential energy becoming kinetic. Then... We were informed the prison was shutting us down.

"I'm sorry, guys, I just, I really don't even know why..." the beautiful, but saddened queen told us.

"Because the devil is supposed to do his job. He's always going to do his job until he expires. His job is to destroy righteousness," Brother Melchizedek said angrily.

"Once you understand the nature of the beast, nothing he does surprises you!" Piper added.

I was upset, bitter even, but I never let it show. I expected this. I just felt sorry for the sister who was obviously blindsided and distraught by the administration's decision. She kept apologizing and we kept assuring her it wasn't her fault. We weren't even allowed to work out in groups of more than four people, I knew this posed an even more serious threat. I wasn't surprised, just reassured the devil existed, but not in the immaterial form that most imagined.

It's amazing how dark times got for me after that. A few weeks after the dismembering of the Men's Growth Group. I was notified by my moth-er that my best friend - Kareem Williams - was murdered. He had been shot in the neck while sitting in his car in a Hall-Manor parking lot. This devastated me and pushed me to writing more. I began immediately to write "Get In, Get Out", a story closely related to our lives and a cautionary tale of deciding to get into the street life and waiting too late to get out. Quite a few stabbings and cuttings took place. A female guard was lacerated by a lovestruck Lifer and had to be transported by helicopter out of the prison. And then, the darkness infiltrated my world.
I worked alongside an older guy named Smitty in the mess hall. We served the trays amongst a few other things. He was a very disrespectful old man. His mouth had no filter and his sexual appetite knew no bounds. I didn't know much about

him, but over time I would learn he had been transferred from another prison for Sexual Deviancy. He had also attempted to rape or molest in past prisons.

One morning, I was fed up with his disrespect, not of me, but others. I told myself If he says or does anything, no matter how large or small, I'll disfigure his face with anything in my reach.

"Fuck you, and your mother!" he yelled at another inmate as they engaged in verbal combat. Not paying attention, his adrenaline made him steer his food cart uncontrollably, nearly running into me.

I said, "Watch where the fuck you're going," in a non-negotiable tone.
"Aw, fuck you, Youngin'..." he said dismissively. My blood began to boil, and my eyes began to scan the kitchen for something I could con-vert into a weapon in a matter of seconds. He came closer to me and said,

"I'll fuck you in your..."

WACK!

I had grabbed an empty water pitcher. I spun to generate more force and it worked. After the contact, all that remained in my hand was the handle. Blood poured immediately and he staggered backwards.

"I'm telling, I'm telling."

I was ready to kill now, but the guys held me back as Smitty fled the area in search of a C.O.; the corner of the hard plastic had caused a serious gash from his right eye to the bottom of the right side of his jaw. Blood flowed over his fingers like a fountain as adrenaline was replaced by nervousness. I sat down and waited for the C.O. to come and escort me to the hole. A guy from Philly sat beside me.

"Listen, Ol' Head's a gipper (Child molester), it's all on his record. When they ask you what happened, you tell 'em he grabbed your ass... You not a faggot, so it don't matter, just tell 'em that. That's your only shot at beating this."

He shook my hand and I nodded.

"Good lookin' out," I said, and he nodded back.

The funny thing is, the C.O.'s didn't come until later that day, when I was back on the cell block.

My name was called out over the loudspeaker and once again, the nervousness returned.

"Hey, what happened in the kitchen today, man?"

I was never a nuisance, so the guard wasn't talking to me as if I was. He seemed to be more concerned with anything.
"Did you clock Old Man Smitty with something, man?"

I could've lied, but it would've done me no good. The place was littered with cameras.

"Yeah..." I admitted.

"What happened?" he asked, disappointment was evident in his tone and facial expression. The disappointment, however, was with the situation – not me. Some people do see the good in you and want you to succeed. It reminded me of my time in Boot Camp at South Mountain. At one point, I began to cut up and my Platoon Commander Lieutenant Dunkel had pulled me to the side.

"Trooper! What the hell are you doing?" he had asked.

"You're not like the rest of these guys. You know your mother came all the way up here just to check on you. She's worried, man. You have a family that cares about you. Some of these kids don't have that. Don't prolong your situation. You have three months and it's over; you only need a couple more credits for your high school diploma. Get it together!"

In that moment, he was no longer the hardened "Jar-head" Marine he had always bragged about being. He wasn't the militant drill instructor we had all grown to fear... He was caring... He was fatherly.

"He tried to touch me..." I told the C.O. in the bubble. It was the truth. He had approached me menacingly and whether his intentions were sexual, aggression, or a mix of both - I didn't know and wasn't about to waste time trying to find out. The guard informed me that they would have to take me to the hole.

"You know I don't really want to," he told me.

"I know, it's all good, man. I made a decision," I told him.

I spent sixty of my ninety days in the hole. After appealing my case, my appeal was finally granted after the review of the details. They even waived the medical bills I was supposed to be paying for the hospital trip and stitches needed for Smitty.

Once I left the hole, I noticed a change within myself. I spoke to Wise about it and he agreed with me. He said he, too, had been feeling a spiritual disconnect for quite some time now as well. No matter how intelligent, our people always had a strong spiritual connection and aware-ness. We've always had some concept of a creator. From Yoruba to Arabia, Sumer to South America - we've never been an Atheistic people - our pineal glands (spiritual antennae) won't allow this train of thought to firmly take root. Learning history was great. Learning science and math was great. Still, my soul had a giant void in it.

I slowly began to gravitate towards the Eastern Schools of thought: Buddhism, Taoism, Jainism, Confucianism, etc. I studied Kundalini Yoga and felt my chakras aligning. My sense of center was prominent. There wasn't a lot of talk of "God" in these ways of life. More, an eliminating of thoughts, words, ideas, and actions that prevented one from drawing close to the source. This decluttering of the mind was exactly the spiritual fix I needed. The last 4-5 years had been spent inundating my mind with facts, data, theories, philosophies, proofs, equations... I needed silence and tranquility.

I now realize Allah was guiding me the entire time. I had to learn these schools of thought for two reasons. To discover remnants of Islam still in pristine form in each walk of life while learning of the adulterated aspects as well. Also, so I could do proper Dawah - calling to Islam. You can't or guide a people if you're not prepared for their rebuttals and what better way to prepare than by becoming a student?

To this day, I am convinced Buddha, Lao Tzu, and many others were, as the Holy Quran says, "messengers sent to their own people", who spoke the language of their people. Torah and Tao mean practically the same thing, the law or way (of heaven). Contrary to popular belief, Lao Tzu, Confucius and Buddha all spoke of "the Deity" (Allah) and "religious duty". They did speak of heaven, hell, the afterlife and resurrection. Disciples tend to water down, or distort, the message of their teachers, but if one

studies, one will realize the Buddha prophesized the coming of Muhammad, as did the Hindus, who refer to him as "Kalki Avatar" as did Jesus in the Gospel of Barnabas. I studied many paths and all roads led to Islam, and the messenger of Islam.
"The religion before Allah (God) is Islam." (Surah 3: Ali 'Imran).

The one thing I started to realize was a lot of religions were named after the prophets, messengers, and gurus that inspired them. Christianity named after the Christ, Buddhism after Buddha, Judaism after Judah, hence they were all "man-made" by disciples and zealots. Not so for Islam. Islam is a word that can be linguistically traced to the world's oldest language and it meant: submission (submission to Allah/God). In the Quran, when Jesus is asked,

"Did you tell the people to worship you?" he replies,

"How can I tell them what I had no right to say?"

This is then repeated regarding all the messengers of Allah, and they all differ and give glory to Allah. Buddha never said enshrine me, deify me, worship statues of me, and make a "new" religion in my name. His teachings were the same as all others: a return to simplicity, a pristine state of mind unadulterated by spiritual pollutants, follow the ways of the Heavens established by Brahma. This is the ultimate truth. All prophets simply remind men to return to Islam (submission) to the will (way) of Allah (descending through the Heavens). From time immemorable by man, this has been "The Language of God".

Two more major events would take place to serve as re- minders to do all within my powers to never return.

"...The skies were misted; wrapped in a thick blanket of dark gray clouds. A slight drizzle, almost dew-like, was falling slowly from those heavy clouds. I could feel it in the air, not the weather but the imminent danger. I walked outside with one of my comrades, expecting something but not exactly what I was about to see. I saw them posted in a military-like phalanx. They were scrutinizing the congested mass of inmates for the enemies. Once they spot- ted them it didn't take long at all. Two groups, one bloods and blood affiliates from New York, Allentown, Buffalo and Reading; the other was a bunch of bearded Muslims from Philly.

Both Groups had soldiers with too much time left in prison to be sane; numbers like life, or a hundred to it. No time to ponder that though... there was a cat-like strike, a razor gashed open some skin, slicing through the ligature of flesh with the ease of a scalpel, the wind, trapped in the open meat blew the epidermis wide open and for a split second I saw teeth and gums like an HD X-ray. Fists flew wildly, blows to the head, then, the bat, the aluminum bat! It swung, missed, then connected with a set of ribs, an arm, a thigh... still the fighting continued. I thought of the 80's movie Warriors, but before I could finish "waaa-ri-or-rrrrs... come out and plaaa-aaay..." The Puerto Rican one, blood affiliated, the one responsible for the blood running from the faces of his enemies, he was on the ground, trapped below a man I used to share a cell with, a blood thirsty killer. Not one of those accidental killers, I mean one who loved to kill, more than he loved money even, a cannon (so he described himself) who at 41 with 40 years left to his minimum and 90 years until his max, is chasing his own death. Suicide, he wants someone to put him out of his misery, but he won't do it to himself, not yet at least, word around the camp is he's dying from AIDS.

He's holding the Puerto Rican down while two of his soldiers, who also happen to be his co-defendants, stop the face of the blood they have on the ground. The kicks are loud thuds, kick, stomp, kick, stomp! I glance around at the spectators, cheering on the raucous, rooting for their favorite gladiator like the coliseums in Rome where this type of blood sport is religiously loved by the blood thirsty men of that time. No coliseums though, no gladiators, just a bunch of brown and black men and a bloody baseball field in the penitentiary.

They kick his face bloody as he twists, turns and struggles to get up. Then the bat again... My old cell mate spots it, picks it up, the killer within dying to be released, dying to let the world see his work, his world being this yard where hundreds of inmates watched in shock. The bat comes down hard, cracks the shins of the Puerto Rican, my own shins feel a tingle as the blood on the ground screams out to his homies, "HELP ME YALL, AHHH, SOMEBODY GET EM OFF ME!!!" There are two holding him down while my old walkie swings the bat hard like Barry Bonds who at the time was at home run #714 the Puerto Rican is crying out for help as they kick his head, punch his head... then...

CRACK

He grabs his face in obvious pain, the crowd moans harmoniously, a loud

"oooooooo" permeates the coliseum. Then,

"Oh shit,"

Some feeling the pain, others just savagely enjoying the show like the vampires in Rome, blood is splashed everywhere like paint, stab wounds in the chest, the abdomen, the neck, black eyes, bruised ribs, cracked legs, fractures, heavy breathing, adrenaline, epinephrine, testosterone... The guards yell,

"DROP THE BAT, DROP THE BAT!!!" they've yet to see the razors...

"GET DOWN! GET DOWN ON THE GROUND! DROP THE BAT! FIRE OFF THE RIFLE!"

But they don't try to break it up. One stands and watches the Puerto Rican take another hard stomp to the face, does absolutely nothing! Maybe some were genuinely scared, they are men, maybe they couldn't stomach all the blood, the savagery, 3 did end up wounded, 2 were stabbed two days prior, some of the guards simply shared the sentiments of the racist guard that watched the bat and foot beat down, screaming for his partner to fire shots into the crowd...

"Josh said the earthquake was a humbling reminder of how fragile and brief our physical lives are."

I read that in a book shortly after the massacre in the yard took place and we were forced to lock down. How coincidental, then again, I don't believe in accidents or coincidences, so how Divine. After we locked in our cells and the adrenaline began to subside, I thought about a re- cent visit with my daughter and mother, I thought about all that I have to live for and that day I realized I wanted to die for a cause because it's so easy to die for nothing. See the massacre stemmed from a man trying to aggressively extend his (secret) homosexuality to his cell mate. The blood affiliated cell mate let his homies know, and they proceeded to protect the honor and manhood of their comrade. Something that small led to a massacre.

I can't prevent death; I can't prevent people wanting to kill me, and I can't prevent my reactions when provoked... but I can eliminate the mediocrity in my live that would lead to petty situations turning big. By focusing on the bigger picture, I won't be caught up in people's bullshit... ***"the earthquake was a humbling reminder of how fragile and brief our physical lives are..."***

Because of this event, the entire prison was locked down, we also had to be searched because of how many weapons had been confiscated during the scuffle. Not only that, the fraternity of correctional officers had been offended because two of their own had been wounded.

This strip search was like no other. The squad that was brought in was made up of officers from all over the state. They were not the prison's staff. They had also come in riot gear and appeared to be trying to provoke sedition to have merit for asserting force upon us. The older inmates called them the "turtle squad" because of their helmets and vests. I simply saw them as extremely threatening.

Once it was time for our cell to be searched, I would see exactly why that premonitory feeling had crept into my heart. I waited outside of the cell in cuffs while my cell mate and companion – M. Manigault was strip-searched. The whole strip- searching process was dehumanizing and emasculating to me. It's a routine I never have and never will get used to.

"Let's go! You're turn!" one of the two dark-spirited officers ordered. I shuffled along - the length of my steps was restricted to the length of the chains I was shackled in - my equilibrium measured by my ability to balance myself with my arms cuffed behind me.

The humiliating routine began.

"Arms out..."

"Palms up..."

"Open your mouth..."

"Lift your tongue..."

"Turn around..."

"Right foot..."

"Left foot..."

"Bend over..."

"Spread your cheeks..."

I lifted myself and shot an angry, questioning glance into the cold blue eyes of the guard conducting the search.

The last demand was never asked, and his mischievous smile let me know he understood he was now going outside of protocol.

"What?!" I shot at him. That rebellion was enough to rouse his aggression.

"Bend the hell over!" he barked.

"C'mon, man," the other guard interjected. "Just do it so we can get this over with..." He was obviously the "good" cop in this scenario.

Again, I bent over, my torso was at a ninety-degree angle to my legs.

"Further!" he ordered. After a minute-long stand-off, he told me to put my clothes back on. I thought my heart would melt due to the raging inferno rising from my solar plex. I stared at him with blood in my eyes.

"Don't fucking stare at me like that!" he said. I never dropped my gaze, but I did smile.

"What's funny?" he questioned, tapping his baton against his palm in a threatening manner.

"You!" I said, knowing that he wanted nothing more than to as- sault me.

"You're a clown," I gritted through my teeth. He heard me but pre-tended he didn't. I remember the minister, Louis Farrakhan, once saying,

> **"When God sends prophets and messengers, they don't care about 'your' power, because they come from 'thee' power.".**

At that moment, I didn't fear him or death.

At that point, his partner – to ease the tension – told me to step outside while the finished the search of the cell. My eyes never left the dirty guard's until he was out of my sight. Mark looked over at me and shook his head. He could see how enraged I was.

The search of the cell was taking abnormally long. I would soon find out why. As the malicious devil in human form stuck his head out of my cell, I noticed a manilla envelope in his hand. It was one of my manuscripts.

"Who's the author?" he asked, smiling roguishly.

"Me," I said, now afraid of what he would do with my work. I had poured my blood, sweat, and tears into those novels, not to mention the time I had spent on them. I'm guessing he had gone through each novel which would explain why the search was taking so long.

"Huh," he chuckled, "One of those smart n...........?" his voice performing a pianissimo before he back into the cell before I could respond. M. Manigault shook his head "no", as if to say, *"don't react"*. We were powerless at that moment.

Finally, it was over, and they told us to go back into our cell. My books were thrown everywhere, but the pages of one novel had been trampled upon by his boots, torn and littered all over.

The title page was right at the door and seemed to be the one that had offended him the most. I read the words:

"Black Girl, White World" By…

The irony was the book's concept was opposite what the title alluded to. It had nothing to do with black subjugation and white privilege. It was about a woman who had perceived the world as racist, but after a few life-changing events, had

come to realize she couldn't condemn an entire race for the sins of a few.
With less than six months left until my release, I was now prepared to re-enter society. The post-traumatic stress induced by the psychological assault of imprison would probably take as long to wear off as it did to form. I accepted this. However, I had all I needed to establish my Limited Liability Company and produce my own books.

By this time, I had approximately four to five fully complete full-length novels along with volumes of essays and poems that could also be converted into books. My mother had completed *"Get In, Get Out"* and saved the Word file for me. She had also contacted J.M. Benjamin, an author out of New Jersey who had received a nice amount of notary thanks to the critically acclaimed novel *"My Manz and Dem"*. We had spoken briefly and would discuss a possible deal once I was re- leased. Sovereignty and autonomy have always meant so much to me, so I knew any deal we did, it would have to be one in which I sustained my independence, preferably a joint venture or distribution deal. Mitanni Publishing was my dream, and nothing would stop its materialization.

The name Mitanni signified my mentality and the mentality I wanted my publishing house to adopt.

I stumbled upon the name during research of Egyptian history and was drawn to it immediately. Mitanni was a small warrior state near the Tigris and Euphrates River. The people were known as Hittites and it was the birthplace of Queen Nefertiti - wife of Akhenaton and Mother of King Tut (Tutankhamen).

Everyone knew of Egypt but not many knew of Mitanni. The warriors from this ancient city would battle with Egypt over control of Syria and though they lost battles, they also won some. I immediately drew a parallel to myself and the authors I would work with. I was a felon now and a minority and entering the publishing world would place me in competition with major conglomerates who were wealthy, well established and world-renowned. Mitanni versus Egypt. Although we would inevitably lose many battles - like the four rejection letters I received from Barnes and Noble before finally being accepted - I was sure we would win some - enough to etch our name in stone and place us in the annuls of history forever.

One author I planned on working with – Abdul – was from Philadelphia. Early on he was one of the first people to believe in me and "see" my vision. He and I would walk to the chow hall together and discuss the state of the publishing industry as well as ideas for future books and potential collaborations. Abdul had life for murder and little to no chance of having the sentence overturned. So, outside of being accepted by an agent or publishing house, he was dependent upon me to get his dreams out.

At one point, M, Manigault had told me it would probably be wise to cut ties with Abdul and end any association I had with him.

"We only talk about books," I promised him, which was the truth. Outside of books we didn't speak about much else. Abdul, however, had taken a liking to me.

One day we walked to the chow hall together and at first all seemed normal. The prison had just shown T.I.'s movie ATL and we were dis-cussing it at length.

As soon as we entered the chow hall, I felt different. I could sense danger but couldn't see it. We were the last to enter the chow hall and for a few paces it remained that way. The next time I looked back, however, there were two men behind us. One a chubby Puerto Rican guy, the other a stocky dark-skinned man. They looked malicious. Their appearance in and of itself was suspicious. We had been the last block to be called for dinner so there shouldn't have been anyone behind us.

They stared us up and down, then walked past us and everyone else in the line. They disappeared but my apprehension didn't.

Abdul and I grabbed our trays and the two guys in front of us sat at our table and continued the discussion about the movie.

"And 'New, New'," one had said regarding Lauren London's character in the movie.

"She's baaaaaaad..." he finished as we all smiled and nodded in agreement. Then my eyes widened as I saw the same dark-skinned man that had followed us into the chow hall stalking towards our table in lion-like fashion. Before I could warn Abdul or say a word, the man rose from his crouching position and stabbed Abdul in his neck, then shoulder, then back. Abdul dropped his hoagie on the floor and as his eyes flew open like a deer spotting a vicious predator, he jumped up and fled for his life.

We all stood up at that moment and when I looked back, the Hispanic guy had his blade pointed at me - prepared to "poke" me if I made any move. He wasn't trying to attack me, however, just keep me at bay in case me and Abdul's association had blossomed into a friendship. I watched as Abdul jumped rails, tables, chairs, and any hurdle he encountered. The Hispanic guy then began to pursue as well. Cutting Abdul off, they stabbed him an- other ten times before the guards were finally able to apprehend them. Abdul had fled the mess hall and, miraculously, hadn't died. "I told you!" Mark said to me angrily.

"I fuckin' told you!" he repeated like an angry older brother, disappointed with his younger brother's naivety.

Later I would find out that the brother of the guy Abdul had murdered had put a hit out on him.

"You gotta be careful who you deal with," Ishmael told me later.

"They was gonna hit you, too, 'Mare, but I told them you really don't deal wit dude like that."

That was it. I really didn't want to speak to anyone else in that jail after that. I didn't know who to trust and didn't want to find out. Luckily, I saw parole a few weeks later and not too long after that I was released.

The day I was released I experienced a myriad of feelings and emotions. Obviously, I was happy to be being released from captivity and wanted to get as far away from prison as possible. I had made friends in this place, however, and it hurt to be leaving them behind; knowing that they would continue to experience all I had - some for the rest of their natural lives.

I was elated to be being reunited with my family - my mother and daughter. I no longer had friends from the outside - outside of Richard and Reggie who, because of their consistent letter writing and support, had now become brothers. Everyone else had left me for dead and though I wasn't bitter, I prayed they didn't expect more than "hi" and "bye" from me. Ronald had left prison about a year before me and though I no longer held animosity towards him, I sure had no plans of spending much time with him. King once told me,

"*You never know how strong your tea is until you put it in hot water...*"

I now knew what he could and could not handle and although I was to blame for who I befriended in life, his statement would never be forgotten. It had been the only piece of evidence the state had against me and outside of the Qadar of Allah, had been the only reason I would end up spending six years in the penitentiary.

I remember leaving with a newfound appreciation for life - in particular - the small things. The only thing on my mind was a warm, home-cooked meal, and a soft bed. I kept imagining how peaceful it would be to use the bathroom without another man in the same vicinity - then how sadly humorous it was that this lost luxury brought joy.

This book could have easily been titled "My Journey to Islam" because, in the end, it was the pursuit of **Sirataal Mustaqeem** (The Straight Path) that had let to, not one, but many revelations of the mind. However, I would not revert - and take my Shahada officially until 2011, three years after being released. When I did, the capstone to my pyramid of knowledge was placed into position.

I left the prison February 28, 2008 with a new sense of purpose, a new diet, an improved physical condition, and a heightened spiritual awareness. For every even that could have led to a racist mindset there was a person placed in my life who prevented my adopting of such a myopic view. Did and does racism exist? Well, of course, it's a spawn of ignorance. As Confucius said, **"Small minds are clannish":** they simply lack a broad enough view of the world to understand, respect, and embrace the cultures, ways, and actions of others. However, I can and will never allow someone else's foolishness to taint the wisdom I've inherited. I am very aware of the enemy, and its evil, often this evil manifest itself in humans, actually – it is the only place it can exist because evil is a designation made by an individual's mind, and there are very few Universal evils (Rape and Pedophilia) everything else is subjective. The rest of creation; the Heavens, Earth, and all life forms between, outside of "man" simply follow the way...

CHAPTER 8

Change

By George Hopkins

I wonder why change was such a hard thing for me to do. Why did I want to continue to indulge in the lifestyle that had gotten me 30 years in prison? If only I knew then, what I know now, I would have changed, but now, it is almost too late.

Change is to cause to be different; to become different or altered; the act, process or result of changing…

Change is inevitable and no matter how much I didn't want to, no matter how much I was stuck in my ways and no matter how comfortable I was, it was something that was imminent. It's either change or find yourself in a perpetual cycle of similar results – failure after failure, negative karma, prison and/or an untimely, disgraceful death.
People fear what they don't understand, and being that change is unknown, it is feared. Change is a road that is seldom traveled – consciously at least – but if I was to follow the course of change

(from a righteous standpoint) the great works would be evident.

I sat down and thought how nature changes on a consistent basis. It rains, hails, snows; there is summer, winter, spring and fall. Just imagine if it stayed hot 24/7 365 days a year with no rain, hail or snow. Let's say, hypothetically speaking, that the summer told the other seasons ,I'm not going to let it rain, hail or snow anymore and I will not let the winter over take my heat`. This would spell disaster for humanity and every other life form on this planet. All because the summer didn't like, or couldn't accept the winter. The oceans, seas and rivers would dry up. Plants, crops and trees would die - along with us!

Fortunately, this isn't the case because nature is in tune with change, but we must take these examples and apply it to our lives where ever we see fit.

CHAPTER 9

Statement of Change
By George Hopkins

Whoever thought I'd be at this point…from a cold savage to God; and the process wasn't easy. I remember saying that I wanted every child to feel how I did and thus came the digression.

From stealing out of stores, lying to whoever was in my face, hating everyone that wasn't me (only to find out later on that I actually hated myself too), wearing a façade of false bravado and machismo, pretending I was tough (or actually feeling tough) to everyone in my face, but deep inside I cried so much that my chest would hurt. I threw rocks at cars, used foul language in my feeble attempt to be grown, got into all types of fights and eventually stopped going to school.

What Was I Thinking?

I smoked weed, but not because I liked it, but instead it was my way of coping with life; my way of escaping reality. Cigarettes, Black and Milds and PCP would follow in succession a few years later. I drank beer and liquor (how could I not do any of this when my father gave it to me religiously?), I also popped pills and sold drugs.

My life began to crumble right before my eyes! If only I could see then, what I see now and view life how I view it now. My brother brought me some information that I couldn't believe. He said I was God.

How could I be God? After all the stuff I did? This was the seed that needed to be planted, even though it wouldn't be watered for many years to come.

In and out of jail I went until one day I had no desire to live. A death wish; if you will. That was the beginning of my transformation. It took me not having anything or wanting anything to begin to focus on self; to begin to break down (to take the head of these four devils) my internal soul and create the God that everyone is searching for. Good Orderly Direction is necessary in striving for perfection, but nothing is easy - so says the Quran,

"Verily We have created man into toil and struggle."
Surah 90

So, struggle is ordained, however, it will eventually bring about ease. So now, I accept all hardship with open arms, knowing that some type of ease will relieve my worries. So, the question, Am I changed? need not be asked. Just watch and my actions will speak volumes about me. Peace!

CHAPTER 10

Desire
By George Hopkins

"Have you seen he who has taken as his god his [own/low] desire, and Allah has sent him astray due to knowledge and has set a seal upon his hearing and his heart and put over his vision a veil? So who will guide him after Allah? Then will you not be reminded?"
Surah [45:23]
-Sahih International

As I read this repeatedly, it became more evident what my problem was, but at first glance - on the surface of these words - my comprehension of this was shadowy (at best). How could a low desire (something that I wanted or longed for) be a god over me/or to me? I wasn't accepting that due to my infantile understanding, and I fought tooth and nail until one day I had to just bear witness to the truth.

I took my low desires and moved them to the forefront not really understanding the cost I was about to pay,

My life!

When I thought back on my history, I saw how remised I was in all my actions, in all my thoughts and in all my decisions.

How could I let my poverty back me into a corner to the point where I could see no light no life or no power, and the only solution for that was money, so that became my savior. I remember praying to God night-in and night-out, and obtaining nothing but hard times, hunger, nakedness, and put out of doors. However, at a young age, I knew that the only thing that could solve this problem was money and the quickest way to get it in my eyes was to break the law and eventually become a parole violator fugitive on the run.

So, I put money before everything that I claimed to love, but tricked myself into believing that I was doing this for my loved ones, to accomplish what I never could accomplish. It was like a dog chasing his tail (we know he's not going to catch it, but still the dog keeps going in circles until he gets tired). In fact, the only thing I did accomplish was going to jail; hurting the people that loved me, and becoming the definition of a deadbeat father. All of this for money. Not knowing (or maybe not caring) that this idol I allowed to become my God could actually save me from nothing!!! It couldn't save me from pain, a lack of love, emptiness, loneliness and so much more! However, it did save me from physical poverty, but in doing so, it took me to the depths of moral corruption, a heartless beast and a down-right evil person which brought me to the worse poverty of all,

A SPIRITUAL POVERTY.

Before I was introduced to marijuana, cigarettes, Black and Milds and wet (PCP), I was formally known as a person with good health. I played sports, and had aspirations of someday going to college to play ball, but when I started smoking weed, the drive I had to play sports came to a halting stop. I mean I still played, but it was obvious that my mind, body, and soul were somewhere else. I was too young to be washed up, but in so many ways I was just like a drug addict who thought that he still had it. And the one thing that I desired the most (from a positive standpoint), which was playing sports and getting out the hood was suddenly stifled by this low desire to get (high). I was chemically imbalanced.

As my lifestyle slowly changed, I no longer went to high school to play ball, but instead, I went to school high! After a few encounters with the law, I was put on parole and when on parole, you are not allowed to smoke weed, but I couldn't stop. It was either stop smoking or go to jail, so I took my chances every- time and anytime I was on parole. Of course, I violated plenty of times, being sent to prison because of my carelessness. Was I really that weak or was the drug just that strong? I eventually started smoking PCP because the P.O. didn't test for this. It was a different high, but I managed, and steered clear from violating. However, I was destroying my life.

When I think back on it, I was no better than the very people I was selling crack to. They had an addiction that they paid for and then I took their money and paid for my addiction. These drugs (my low desires) became my God and ruled me. And it's safe to say that I couldn't function without them. I once read, **the body is the temple of God and that Spirit of God dwelled in you.**

Now if this was true, then this means that I was destroying the house that God lived in, and if he lived there didn't that mean we were one in the same? So now, I ask how this low desire could be God over the God in me. Of course, it couldn't be, but what it boils down to is a war between two wolves in my body - one good and the other bad. Whichever one I fed the most always won the battle. I think it's paramount to say that I only feed the god within now.

So now, I ask you to recollect seeing what (if any) low desires that you have and strive no to let them become a God over you.

CHAPTER 11

Plan to Improve
By George Hopkins

I plan to improve by not only changing my outlook on how I see life, but also by implementing these things in my everyday walk. I adopted 12 principles to guide me through the Valley of the shadow of death. These principles are

"Knowledge, wisdom, understanding, freedom, justice, equality, food, clothing, shelter, love, peace and happiness."

I had to learn that the most important person in the universe is ME! I beg that you don't look at this as being selfish. The reasons why I started thinking this way is because I learned that the first law of nature is ‚self- preservation`, meaning that I had to save self before I could save anyone else…

By continuously striving, perfection will be met in no limit of time. Change is the course that needs to be followed, but from a production output. Time reveals all things, so within that matter, all will fall into place…. Responsibility must be established or all that is done will be in vain. Responsibility is your ability to respond to pressure positively. When we

accomplish this, discipline is the outcome. The word you find in discipline is disciple, and of course there were twelve. The number twelve represents, love, and that is the only way to improve, by having love for you. So, if you love yourself you will go through hell to make it right. Or in this case…

IMPROVE.

I hope that whoever is reading this is in a very peaceful state (mentally and physically). All that I ask is that you follow my lead when comprehending my words. Nothing in life is easy; nothing worth having anyway! So why is it that we constantly search for the easy way out or for the easy things in life? I'm used to hearing people complain about how hard it is in their life and I've done the same up until now.

There's a saying that goes adversity defines true character' and if this is the case what kind of people are we?

Better yet, what type of man am I to succumb to the pressure of the world?

Things that come to mind are weak, impatient, unintelligent, a follower and so on.

These can all be corrected once we learn (and accept), that struggle is ordained for all of us. What do you mean that struggle is ordained? I'm saying that it is inevitable; it's going to happen whether we want it to or not. So, it's best to get prepared for the storm.

However, the storm manifest (within) first, so the inner self is the most important to be assayed. Mastering the internal wars takes precedence over everything else - especially when you understand that everything comes from within!

Even the Holy Quran backs up what I'm saying in its writing ch.94:5-6: **surely with difficulty is ease, with difficulty is surely ease.**

> **Indeed, with hardship [will be] ease.**
> [Surah 94:5-6] Sahih International

This shows and proves that hardship is a part of life, but it does not go without notice for every hardship an ease comes about.

Follow my lead for a second. When a person works out (physical training) a struggle takes place, difficulty and/or hardship - be it calisthenics, resistance weights, push- ups, pull ups - etc. The ease that comes after is how your body feels when you are finished - its extreme beauty - i.e.

Good healthy heart rate that beats with tremendous power, which will enable oxygen to circulate throughout your body and bloodstream. You will be healthy and at the very least have a stunning body. Or just think about the planting of a seed into fertile soil. The seed which is alive (whether we recognize this or not is a different story) is in a dormant stage and has to be kick - started (if you will) from the pouring of water. The water to the seed is like a fibrillator to a man who has flat-lined.

Once it seeps through the shell the seed has the hard task of pushing its fragile roots, not only through the shell itself, but through the tough, rough and rocky soil.   Which is not easy at all, but the seed never complains. Once firmly rooted in the soil, it has the job of pushing up through the earth at which time the ease comes. The Ease…. The Joy…. Happiness….in this case is synonymous to the beauty we see from the seed which has grown to become a lovely tree, plant, flower - etc.

History shows that in order for ease, happiness, beauty, etc., to come about, hardship, difficulty, pain and whatever else relates to these worlds has to happen…

All the great people before me; Jesus, Moses, Abraham, Martin Luther King, Harriet Tubman, Rosa Parks (and so many more). They all experienced grief, dismay, sadness or death, but the reward afterwards can be equated to heaven.

So, who am I to expect anything less than what they went through? I think that is selfish. Complaining about a situation never makes it better. You think I'm not unscrewed immensely at the fact that LEGALLY, I'm a slave according to the 13th amendment? Or what about the fact that my support system ceases to exist, in fact I'm being treated as if I never existed!!! So, I have no money, food, or hygiene. Can you imagine being locked up for 9 years and having no one to write, call, or email? Having no pictures, getting no visits and the woman that claims she loves you is loving another man? All this hurts, but nothing more than the realization that I know my cell mates better than I know my own children! That my children (under the carless supervision of their mother), are being raised by every, and any man in their mother's life; calling that man dad and whatever else, which is something I would never allow my children to do under my guidance. Now that's pain!

This may be the deciding factor on why so many people go out and commit crimes again. Can you imagine being left for dead, by everyone that claims to be family or friend, only to survive in the end?

Having people that you don't know, who more than likely hate you because of the color of your skin, treat you less than a man, talk down to you, deny your visits, set you up; lie on you, lock you in for nothing, beat on you etc. Plus, not having a woman (who is the embodiment of heaven) to talk to, to touch, kiss, rub, to   SEX, LOVE, HOLD; TO SMELL (not only the fragrance she wears, but her natural Divine scent). When all of this is snatched from a man it leads us straight to savagery and once there many never recover. The hardest thing for us to do is get out of prison because they (the powers that be) design this so that we are always one step from failure - not to mention that they don't want to let us go anyway. The second thing is adapting to society. This is not a cake walk either, being that we have every element in the physical world working against us. But knowing what I know now, I welcome the pressure that the world has to offer - not because I enjoy hardship, but instead because of the diamond I will become once I see through it all. In addition, once I see through it, I will feel like Kanye West…. You can't tell me nothing?

Peace

CHAPTER 12

Fighting
by George Hopkins

Contrary to popular belief, not everyone is a fighter, and it is easy for me to say that not all people like to fight. At least I was not a fighter, so you know I did not like to fight. However, that quickly changed. Especially growing up in a neighborhood where children were encouraged to fight (physically) to survive. Therefore, they picked on children less fortunate, smaller than them, weaker than them. Not to mention the video games that displayed nothing, but killing, gun shooting, and destruction. Including the television, that portrayed the same thing. Because of these images projected into my mind's eye, I began to see fighting a little bit different - as if it was okay to do - I mean why else would they have it on every television station, in every movie, in every video game and in damn near all music? Whether it was the good guys or the bad guys, fighting or killing was the result. Once planted into my subconscious mind these images would re-surface every so often, which produced a violent act on my part.

However, what goes unnoticed is the hidden hand that brings all this about.

There was a book written by Iyanla Vanzant called ,The Spirit of a Man`, in which she said on page 210,

"That universal law responds to the energy of our consciousness by creating circumstances and situations that mirror the mental and emotional energy we send forth."

After reading what she wrote, and applying it to what I have seen and been through, I now can understand why the world is the way it is and why I went through what I went through.

There have been numerous situations in the past of mass murders. Senseless acts committed by individuals whom they determine, in most cases, to have mental disorders, and in some cases, they have no answer at all.

However, could the universal law that Ms. Vanzant was speaking about hold any weight to today's tragic events? I think so.

As the years came and went, I managed to become a thug, a savage, a beast with very little remorse for anyone and it seemed that I liked it. It brought excitement to my life. Let me explain: At one time, some friends and I got high off stealing cars. This was a major thing and we did it every day. We knew that we could be arrested, but we did not care. Even worse, death from behind the wheel - as we were constantly in high- speed chases. I remember one day that I was in a high-speed chase in the summer of 2000. I was riding in a Lex Truck smoking heavy weed, music blasting, and making crack sales as if the law never existed. The owner, whose wife ended up reporting it stolen, lent this particular truck to me,

I lived for the car chases, shootouts, fights and whatever else that complimented the streets. Therefore, when this occasion arose, I was up for the challenge. Driving down the block in Harrisburg, PA, I noticed two police cars following me and even though I was dirtier than Fred Sanford (carrying drugs, guns and paraphernalia), I secretly hoped that they would hit the lights. Of course, they did. I went from zero to 90 quicker than an addict could pull from his stem. I literally smoked the cops and was smooth sailing.

However, I know as everyone else does that you cannot outrun the police radio, so I had to get somewhere fast. There were cops everywhere, in every direction, and while I had a good lead on them, there were coming.

At this time, I was up to 100 mph in this small city, and it was on a Sunday. This is important because as I am speeding (so high that it looked like I was driving in slow motion) there is a little girl of about 7 years in age who is crossing the street to go to church.

However, she is oblivious of me, and I am now at a crossroad! Do I hit her and keep going (just to avoid prison) or do I hit the break, flip the truck, and ultimately kill myself? My mind was set - as I flashed back to, New Jersey Drive - smiling to myself like I am too superb a driver and skillful enough to dodge her and make the great escape I was putting together. To make a long story short, I did not hit her, but I did go to jail and this is one example of how I did bad and evil or harmful things just for the love of it.

As I began to learn more in life, I found out that I am not the only one who knows that a thing can be bad, harmful, or evil to self and still do it!

For example, doing drugs, knowing it can kill and will destroy the mind, the body, and soul. Using excessive seasonings on our food as if you will not get high blood pressure (and that is if you do not already have it). Smoking cigarettes thinking that we cannot get lung cancer; breaking the law like there is no justice system in place just for that. However, why is this? I heard that we are easily, led in the wrong direction, and it is hard, to be led in the right direction. While reading the Holy Quran, I stumbled upon a scripture that made it plain.

In 2:216 it says

> **Fighting has been enjoined upon you while it is hateful to you. But perhaps you hate a thing and it is good for you; and perhaps you love a thing and it is bad for you. And Allah Knows, while you know not.**
> *[Surah 2:216]*
> *-Sahih International*

This is the science of all my problems right here.

Fighting depends upon you and the first (and most exigent) fights start within self. We must be able to overcome our own twisted and wicked machinations! If we do not, we will forever continue to indulge in things that are contrary to righteousness, civilization and the most important - LIFE, and we will love every second of it.

CHAPTER 13

Influence
By George Hopkins

One of the main things that influenced me growing up in the late 80's and early 90's was rap music. Of course, at the time, and for a long time, I was oblivious to it. As I look back on my life and the transformation that it took on, it is easy to see the connection between the two.

I rushed to the music stores every month to spend my parent's hard-earned money on these rappers: N.W.A., Mobb Deep and Bone Thugs and Harmony, Jay-Z, Biggie, 2 Pac, DMX, The Lox, Redman, Snoop Dog, Ice Cube, Scarface, and a whole slew of other rappers.

Rappers that I deemed to be nice, and they were at their particular craft, but none had any substance, consciousness, or positivity for the children.

Some say, So what? or What does this have to do with anything? Well, for a while — since I can remember — there was a saying that **ART IMITATES LIFE** and this held true for some time up until **LIFE STARTED IMITATING ART**. Yes, rap is a form of art as is all music.

What happened was rappers were imitating so-called gangstas and thugs in the streets, and that is not to say some of them were not in the streets, but they took their admiration of these criminals with their criminal acts and put it on paper, then pushed it out through in their music. Then what happened was the younger generation that got a hold of these tapes and c.d.'s, whose minds were so fertile, began to take on these roles rapped about in the music.

Thus, the role reversal was complete. Rap is one of the strongest voices of the people, and obviously, these musicians did not know the power of their music, either that or they did not care.

...Follow my lead

Growing up, I never heard the word nigga until I started listening to rap music! I had no idea such a word existed, nor did I know what it meant. Even though we used this word as a term of endearment, I did not know that this word was high-jacked from an era in history, from a group of people that used the original word (nigger) as a way to degrade black people by calling them ignorant, a dead people, stupid and less than human! Nigga quickly became a part of my vernacular as it did with every other child my age. I could not understand for the life of me why adults (with the slightest amount of sense) would always cringe or correct us (children) when we used that word.

Rappers made it cool to go against the law; to go against our parents; to go against righteousness. They glorified the fast life; selling and using drugs, killing people, nice cars, pretty women, prostitution, going to jail, hating the police, and doing whatever is necessary to get ahead - no matter the cost. They made it seem as if this was the only way, and it is safe to say, That I was brainwashed. I was calling women bitches, hoes, and whores; having sexcapades: making them do things they did not want to do; treating them just like the concrete I walked on. It did not bother me one bit - not even when I thought of the fact that I had a mother, grandmother, sisters, and a daughter who were all queens in my eye.

I was convinced that selling drugs was the best way to make real money (little did I know that the average drug dealer barely makes minimum wage (sometimes less) when it is all said and done). Therefore, I sold drugs without a second thought about the children who would be hungry, who would be homeless, or without clothes due to their parent's addictions. I even had sex with some of these women, I dare say was clean and disease free in exchange for drugs.

I never shot and killed anybody, but the intentions in my heart got me convicted the same way I would have, had I actually succeeded in my attempts. This does not mean I am not a murderer. Every time I sold drugs, I took a part of someone's life; a part of someone's soul; their intelligence, morals, love, dignity. I was ultimately killing them softly. I sit down and think how many times I murdered the happiness of someone's child because of my own selfishness. I think about the way I may have helped to kill someone's relationship, someone's dreams, aspirations, or the way I essentially committed homicide on the bond my children and I would have had due to my incarceration.

Going to jail was like the rite of passage according to these rappers - if not consciously definitely unconsciously.

This is what solidified your spot (if you will) as a hard-core street dude. To come home from jail, without snitching, was the last piece of the puzzle. It let everyone know that you were real, thorough, or a person who could be trusted. In most cases, it was like a holiday when you came home: drugs, drinks, parties, guns, women, money, clothes, and cars - etc. All to bring you back into the fold of the very thing that took you out of it. Where is the intelligence in that?

Damn near every rapper smoked weed or drank alcohol. This was the *in thing* to do so of course I followed their footsteps. I wanted to be so much like these dudes, that I actually was smoking weed before I even knew how to inhale! Crazy, right? No, I did not know how to inhale, but the dudes I was smoking with saw me wasting their precious

marijuana, and they quickly taught me the art of smoking. I became very proficient. I tried to capture everything I heard in the music from partying, clubbing, tricking, not going to school, fighting - everything (they) called real! Boy was I taught. In fact, I probably was influenced more (by my own people) than what happened in the 1700's and 1800's.

Being from the hood, (as we so eloquently put it) made it that much more easier to dislike/hate the police, but to get if from your people in the music you loved to hear added so much more spice to it. It was like on sight with me. Any and every time I saw the police -whether they were kicking in a door or saving someone's life - the same feelings would arise that the cat and dog, or cat and mouse had for each other.

I am fully aware that some of the characteristics that may have led to a, way of life for others and me may come from different roots, and if this were the case, rap music would have to be the water that helped these roots grow. These rappers, who say that they're not role models (or that they did not ask to be one), have to know that children and in some cases young adults, look to them for many things, i.e., fashion, new and cool language (ebonics), how to treat women, and anyone else in their life. They paid attention to how the rappers made money and so much more that you could not even imagine.

Knowing this, wouldn't it be wise to encourage our youth - the very ones who are to lead the future - in the way of civilization, righteousness and spirituality? It is our duty to encourage our youth in anything other than evil, wickedness, and immoral acts.

Well, some rappers do rap in a positive way, but they hardly get any recognition because record companies will continuously shuffle your album to the back, until you get with the program. What I would like to say to these rappers that sell their soul for the sole purpose of popularity and money is parallel to what Jesus said to his disciples in Matt. 16:26, ***for what profited a man, if he shall gain the world, and lose his own soul?***

I would like to challenge these rappers to see who can make an album (not a song) that has some type of substance in it. Alternatively, are they too disinclined to give a thought doing it? You bare a heavy load when you put that microphone in your hands and I do not want my children to grow up wanting to be drug dealers, gang bangers, womanizers, or drug users because of something they heard in your music. You have an opportunity to redeem yourself by helping to save our future generations. Please do not let us down! Remember, if WORDS CAN HEAL, THEY CAN DEFINITELY KILL...

P.E.A.C.E

CHAPTER 14
Patience
By George Hopkins

To have patience is to become a patient in your walk of life and the only medical treatment is your endurance which will crystallize your understanding and character giving you the virtue that is needed to keep on pushing.

Everything starts with patience or at least it should. Patience means to endure trouble, hardship, annoyance, or delay without complaint or anger.

...Persevering

...Persistent

I always heard that ,Patience is a virtue' I continuously repeated it without knowing the true meaning of it.

Virtue means moral excellence and righteousness; goodness!

Now that I know that, shall I continue? So much of my problems, trouble, pain, hardship, annoyance and anger came from rushing into things without contemplation, without taking time to rationally put my thoughts together. The great enemy of patience is instant gratification. For whatever reason we as a people, want things when we want them instead of working for them and being patient. So many times throughout our lives, this is the reason why we fall short of our greatest potential.

There is really no reason to rush into anything because when this is done intelligence is not included. This is one of the reasons I was breaking the law instead of working. I was running myself into an early grave because I was not living correctly. This is the reason why my children are growing up in a single parent household instead of with both parents.

Patience is something that cannot be forced on you, but it has to be learned, it is almost like a necessity of life.

...Follow my lead

Some many times in life we accept things that we see, or hear, on face value instead of breaking down all the information; instead of doing our own investigating; instead of …… Well, you get the point. When we take this approach, we do ourselves a grave disservice, and this goes unnoticed, but only to the individual who is easily swayed.

...Good things only come

I remember when I first heard this slogan
,GOOD THINGS ONLY COME
TO THOSE WHO WAIT'. I will latch on to it the same way a baby does his mother's nipple when feeding I used this slogan so loosely - along with everybody else - not fully understanding the meaning or what I was prescribing to the people listening, but it was merely out of ignorance. One day I sat down
and asked myself, ,how could anything good come to anyone who just sits back and waits for it to come -with no work whatsoever? That's so close to an oxymoron I can't tell the difference. In life you have to work for everything - be it money from a job, nice body, strong mind, a nice home, beautiful and successful children, righteousness, civilization, refinement, a good man or woman - etc. The Bible says ,You reap what you sow Gal. 6:7, so if you put in no work that's exactly what you'll get in return...

NOTHING!

Does that make sense to the person reading this? While going through the Quran, I found that it says the same thing - just in different words. In 53:39-40 it reads ,and that man can have nothing, but what he strives for, and that his striving will soon be seen`. Now both of these books can't be wrong, or is it me?

What I came to realize is that...

GOOD THINGS ONLY COME TO THOSE THAT (WORK) FOR IT.

I hope that you can see my angle and agree with me? Now if you can, let me be the first to say that I'm working for this (for us); that I'm working to get my family back, to get my home, but if I haven't put in enough work (don't worry kids) because I plan to give it all that I have and all within my power to live to see the day when you can wake and go to sleep safe, sound and with a smile on your face.

Now if that isn't good enough, I plan to work like a woman does when she is in labor; like there is no tomorrow; just like Harriet Tubman did when she was freeing the slaves!

The formula for ,work is FORCE times DISTANCE, and force is how heavy a thing is, and the speed it travels. Distance is how far it goes. So work is heavy, and moves at a certain speed for a certain amount of time - thus producing the desired outcome. And if you're waiting for something, then you are not in accordance with the formula!

Then I thought about this slogan TIME IS MONEY, and this sounded so slick rolling off the tongue that I used it for everything. Then one day, I had to face the music that ,money would never be equated to time'.

I went through all the justifications I could think of, and they all pointed to this one thing: That you make money according to the time you put in. So, the question I asked was which one was more valuable, Time or Money? I would have to say that if someone is willing to pay you (a small amount of money to them) for the time you invest for them (which is going to produce millions for them) then your time is much more valuable. If you cannot see that, look at it from an angle that people are willing to pay for your time because they know what it will produce; that no matter how much money you lose, you can always get it back, but when you ever lose time, you can never get it back. That's the difference (a big difference might I add) between the two. That's where the saying ,if I could rewind the hands of time' comes into play, but it cannot be done, showing and proving the value of time. So always use it wisely because you will hate to look up one day and wonder, where the hell all the time went?

CHAPTER 15

What's the Value in a Name?
By George Hopkins

If words can heal and words can kill, is there any value in a name, which for all intent and purpose is a word?

Names are giving to describe or represent something - from the characteristics they possess - and when it's in reference to a human the names hold so much more weight.

So, it is important to choose the names for ourselves and children carefully, because your name gives you a legacy to live out.

Every race of people on the planet has a name that is consistent with their history and ancestors except the black man and woman in North America.

Why is that? Well first and foremost they were stripped of their name (while in slavery) and given the name of their particular slave owner, and we still carry this name today, but this was more than just to identify them, it was to keep them from knowing who they truly are and where they came from.

The pages history - especially the Bible - shows that whenever a person has reached a certain plateau in their spiritual growth that another name is bestowed upon them to live through.

The most notable are Abram to Abraham, Saul to Paul and Jacob to Israel.

John 1:4 said **, the word became flesh and dwelled among men** meaning that it was brought to life through actions and deeds, so to it is the same for the names we are given - be it apart of your essence or contrary to it. So, choose wisely.

This mind is like a parachute, and if open it will save you, but if closed it will kill you! So do yourself a favor and open up your mind to this analogy I'm about to give. Now of course this hypothetical and I beg that you entertain it for the sake of this writing.

Imagine taking a puppy from out of the womb of its mother, and not only calling it a cat, but treating it as such.

After a while, the dog would be so confused that it too, would believe that it was a cat-basically other than self.

Because of the way we treated it, the puppy would eat cat food, try to climb trees, use the litter box, and even try to meow. John spoke in the Bible of this power.

It is conducive to have a name that is consistent with your character and

God, because as the Bible says in Proverbs 18:21 **death and life are in the power of the tongue**, so wouldn't it be wise to have a righteous name of God opposed to anything contrary?

That is the questions that all should think about….I know I have!

CHAPTER 16

Natural vs. Normal
By George Hopkins

According to the Webster Dictionary, natural means - based upon the innate moral feelings or inherent sense of right and wrong held to characterize mankind.

Normal means - according to, constituting, or not deviating from an established norm, rule or principle: conformed to a type, standard or regular pattern.

After reading these definitions and applying them to today is society and myself, I see a lot wrong between the two.

As for me, everything I did was normal, and never natural, but that's because I was easily deceived at a young age that the life I was living was correct. I now know that was a lie. In my neighborhood, struggling with bills, rents, clothes, cars, getting a job, keeping a job, even struggling in school was normal. This is what pushed most of us to eventually start selling drugs!

So being in the streets became normal for me - buying, cooking and selling crack cocaine was done so often where I lived, to not see it would alarm anyone - even productive citizens. Along with this lifestyle came drug usage (weed and alcohol). In my family this was socially accepted. I mean my father gave me

wine, beer and any other type of alcohol just because. So again, I grew up with the idea that it was okay to use. Going to prison even became the norm where I'm from (and now that's where I sit).

Now in no way am I pointing the finger, or trying to judge, anyone with that I'm writing, but instead, my aim is to shed light where it's most dark. It seems that we somehow got these two words mixed up with each other. This has happened because we have unconsciously accepted what the world has said to be right, as the truth, and that has put us in direct controversy with God himself!

If we claim to be followers of Jesus, then we have to apply what he taught and make the same hard decisions he made regardless of how the world feels about it. Contrary to what we may want to believe, this is not a popularity contest, and many can bear witness that

Jesus wasn't popular or he wouldn't have been murdered by the very government that was set to protect the land.

Jesus said to ,be in the world, but not of the world' and this is because you cannot serve two masters at the same time, so of course, your body will be in the world, but your mind has to be that of God! Follow me?

Why is it that everything God says don't do, the world says to do and we follow the world instead of God? This has become the norm and with most of us, but we don't see it, and since we don't, I'll bring light to some of the situations. I hope that you can see my point of view.

In the book of Genesis 19:1-38, God set out to destroy a whole city for what was called an abomination in the sight of God. Homosexuality. He (GOD) told Abraham, if he could find five (5) righteous people in the city that he would spare the whole town. However, he could not find one righteous person, so the town was destroyed! Even killing the wife of Lot for looking back at the city, after she was told not to look back when they were running for refuge. It wasn't only because she looked back but because her looking back was a sign of her not only being in the world, but of the world.

Fast forward to today and the world/government/and people in it not only accept the very thing that got a whole city destroyed, but some even participate in this abomination.

In knowing that the first law of nature is SELF PRESERVATION one of the best and most satisfying ways to do this is by abiding to the second law of nature which is to PRO-CREATE. The only nature way for this to happen is with a man and woman, but never with two of the same sex! Unless again, you just want to be normal, you can try the cloning thing which is definitely unnatural.

What about the way we use the words like bitch, hoe, whore, slut, and chick? We use these words so loosely when referring to women. I hear this so much that I have concluded that these are the only words, (actually misnomers) to describe a woman, but what about words like QUEEN, PRINCESS, MOTHER, HONEY, LOVE, SWEETY, BUTTERFLY, WIFE, and STARSHIP. But again, this has become the norm thanks to society! So now we have young ladies growing up thinking that it's okay to be called these names so much that they now refer to themselves as such, like it's a rite of passage.

We NEED TO CHOOSE OUR WORDS CAREFULLY WHEN ADDRESSING OUR WOMEN.

I say that because **A NATION CAN RISE NO HIGHER THAN ITS WOMAN** (Elijah Muhammad). So, if that's the case, and it is, the women are our best asset to changing the future for the good! History teaches that for every no-good woman there's a no-good man that made her that way (E.M.), because she is a reflection of him.

Or just think about the slogan ,sex sells' which manipulated the people (men and women) into turning our beautiful young girls into sex symbols. This is not natural-where our women starve themselves (which is unhealthy) to achieve the Hollywood look. They walk around with next to nothing on, revealing everything on their body, that's supposed to be sacred and exclusively for a husband, to the world. And we (men) are no better because we promote it like a savage beast sitting with our tongues out like a thirsty dog. From surgery, liposuction, breast, lip and butt implants are all normal but none of it can change nature, for when father time calls, your body will obey!

Getting old is natural - also beautiful because it shows your progress at different stages in your existence. It's like when a tree begins to lose its leaves because of the sudden change in weather. The leaves start to change colors, but these colors aren't ugly. They have their own appeal - even to the person that hates the winter.

It's imperative that we get out of this world (mentally, spiritually and emotionally), but in doing so we will be looked at like we are crazy. Case in point is what Peter said in 1st Peter Chapter 4: **PREPARE YOURSELF TO THINK IN THE SAME WAY CHRIST DID.** You have spent enough time in the past doing what ungodly people choose to do. You lived a wild life. You longed for evil things. You got drunk. You went to wild parties. You walked in lust. You worshipped statues of God.
UNGODLY PEOPLE THINK THAT IT'S STRANGE WHEN YOU NO LONGER JOIN THEM IN WHAT THEY DO. SO THY SAY BAD THINGS ABOUT YOU. (The Honorable Elijah Muhammad)

Seems like he was talking to us today if you ask me. But who am I but a messenger to the people who want to look, listen, learn and observe.

CHAPTER 17

The Butterfly Effect
By George Hopkins

When an individual is afforded the opportunity to experience transformation from a positive standpoint, it's a beautiful thing, because not only are they changing for the good and betterment of society, but they'll be able to see their faults; mistakes and bad characteristics for what they really are and use them to rebound off of.

Just think about the caterpillar - whose essence is a beautiful butterfly - but can't transform into its natural form until undergoing whatever is necessary to transcend. The caterpillar is a wormlike, often hairy insect larva that is considered to be unattractive to almost everyone on the planet. However, the caterpillar has the ability to wrap itself up in a cocoon which is a case usually of silk formed by the insect, and in this cocoon, (protective shield) the change begins.

...My caterpillar stage

I came into this world with nothing and it got worse and worse as I got older. I couldn't figure out why we had no food; why I had to wear my brother's clothes, (which were too big) to school; why my parents were drug addicts; why x-mas was only a thought in my mind, but never a reality. What was it that I done to this God that everyone prayed to? Did he even exist? And if he did, he had to have a sick twisted idea of what humor was to continue to allow this to happen. These were some of the thoughts that dominated my brain.

It was once said that **all you need to change the future is the mind of a child.** This might be the reason why the world is how it is now. Because the people of my age, were cultivated, in the wrong area of things when we were children.

Have you seen him who takes his low desires as God?

When I got old enough to fend for myself, that's exactly what I did! I aimed to get everything I didn't have as a child, (by any means necessary) and I saw nothing wrong with it. While some may say ,it's hard to not see your wrongs, or your sins, I differ in opinion because when you're blind, deaf and dumb to the truth, YOUR JUST THAT!

Try to see it from this angle, where the Holy Quran says, **the life of this world is made to seem fair to those that disbelieve**. Now, if this script holds any validity, then the world (as I've seen it) was fair, (meaning ok). And if the world itself sees what's transpiring as fair then we're all a part of the disbelievers. So, when my father gave me alcohol and wine to drink it was okay; it was looked at as cute to see a 4- and 5-year-old tipsy.

When I began to smoke weed and skip school my popularity heightened. It heightened so much that the girls my age were compelled to have me sexually, which went straight to my head, but before then, they had no desire to be with me what-so-ever.

Everyone my age sold drugs, carried pistols, stole cars, was having sex, used drugs, went to clubs, stayed out all night and so much more. I mean you almost had to be accepted. It became second nature to me. It didn't matter that I was hurting myself, (mentally as well as physically), hurting my family and of course my victims from a direct result of selfishness.

There's nothing new under the sun, and trust me I did it all. I did it so much that I was tired of living it, but what else could I do, (being that this was all I knew) except wish for death?

Wishing for it in such a manner that I began planning it, but why wish for death when I had so much to live for? Was it because of my childhood?
Because I was on so many drugs, (weed, ecstasy, PCP, alcohol) that I could not cope or function properly? Because I did not accomplish what I set out to do in life? Because I felt like a failure?
Because I had no real money? Because I lost the only woman I truly loved?
Because I wanted to meet this God that I couldn't see while alive? Because.....

Well, I can imagine that all these played a part in my decision to see death around every corner I turned! I sometimes tricked myself into believing that, (I was death itself) and hope and prayed that I could bring me to some un-lucky soul. When I actually thought about it, I had too much pride to take my own life, but then I figured maybe - just maybe - I could put myself in a position to have someone else take my life for me! No matter how sane I thought it was, it was the most irrational thing I ever thought of.

Needless to say, that the plan didn't work because I'm sitting here writing this to you, but in a sense it did, it just wasn't physically. See, I died inside on 9/13/05, which is the exact date of my mother's birthday, and when I almost took another man's life which ultimately landed me here in prison. I hoped for the life of me that this man had a gun so that I could go out in a blaze of glory, but he didn't.

The cocoon: While being in prison I couldn't do anything, but face myself (and that was an ugly sight to see). I had to deal with me, and in doing so, I had to turn to where everything originated - and that is inside.

The questions that came to mind were: *How did I get to this point in my life? What am I going to do now? How will I survive? Why am I still alive?*

Why did I want to die anyway? Who am I? What about my children? Did I really love them? Am I a coward? Weak? -- And if so, why? My favorite questions were, ,how the hell am I going to get out of here?

As I wrestled with these questions, I slowly began to try and put my life back together, and just like a 1000-piece puzzle, it took time, dedication and discipline. I began to program within the jail, learning what I could, no matter how obsolete the program was. I tried keeping family ties close together, but to no avail. I studied the law as much as possible, so that I would have a fighting chance. Years later, I learned that the studying of the law was almost all for nothing because the Government doesn't follow the law that they make unless it is applicable for them.

I was a long way from where I am now, as I continued to still dibble and dabble in negative things within the prison society: drugs, alcohol, fights and much more. Slowly, but surely the façade I created while living in the streets began to crumble right before my eyes. Not only was I avoiding negativity, but I was also thinking clearer, much more civilized. I was quick to listen and slow to talk. My heart was even softer and I was able to come up with a solution for a problem before the problem ever came about. I learned to be compassionate; I even cried throughout this whole experience which was something unheard of for me.

And thus, a beautiful butterfly emerged, still having faults, but being able to master them on the spot - which was a testament to my hard work. I'm continuously striving for perfection every second of the day (physically and mentally), and being willing to help people when they're in need of it shows my progress in becoming a civilized person. I began to read more to strengthen my knowledge and vocabulary. This is important because it is said (according to the Bible, that **my people are destroyed for a lack of knowledge** and in another place that **the tongue is the most wicked thing in the body**, so to conquer these two feats produced a much better man; a person who now opts to think first and then think again before reacting.

When I sit back and think about my uphill climb, (my transformation) I'm amazed, but not at the journey: the bumps, bruises, the highs and the lows, but instead the reaction I received from my peers. Who, for some reasons, seem like they were very angry about me changing for the positive then continuing to do negative stuff. I couldn't understand it until I read 1st Peter 4:4, now I can see why I was liked more when I was a savage opposed to now. If that's not an oxymoron, I don't know what is. Then I thought like to hell with them anyway because

I'D RATHER BE HATED FOR DOING WHAT'S RIGHT, THEN LOVED FOR DOING WHAT'S WRONG!

CHAPTER 18

Let Go to Move Forward
By George Hopkins

I was reading something from out of the Five-Percenter newspaper today that sparked what I am writing now, and it made me reflect on life as a whole, but also introspectively. The latter is the most imperative because self-analysis and self-examination are the basis for self-correction. In addition, might I add that at some point in time in everyone's life, the betterment of self should be top priority? Instead of worrying about what lies ahead, I decided to revisit my past to precisely calculate what led up to my future (which is now my present) being so grim.

I remember my ever-so-precious mother crumbling right before my eyes due to her addiction to drugs. There were times when my Black Goddess never came home (which would put my brother and me in a position that no child should ever be in, that of survival by sheer instinct). Looking at what I went through up that point in my life (age 5), I made a jejune decision (based off emotions) to sell drugs because I wanted to have money. I never wanted to want for anything again in life; I hated being poor, not having any food, clothes, or Christmas toys. Most of all, I just wanted every child to feel how I felt!

I think it's important to mention that as my mother got her life together, mine was spiraling out of control. That's why, for this reason and this reason alone, should we be ever-so-mindful of our ways and actions in front of the child who at this tender age - is impressionable and easily impregnated with the seeds (be it good or bad) from their parents/guardians.

To keep the story moving along, let's just say that everything I learned as a child played a major role in my success and/or demise as I got older. Better yet, it was my demise more than anything and success was a long shot.

I sold my first drug (with the help of my brother) at the age of 14, and bought my first gun when I was 15 years young. This is important to mention because at this time, I was still active in school, and a pretty good basketball player who had dreams of going to college one day. This was the turning point for me, or the fork in the road in which I chose to travel the path of least resistance. In no limit of time, I was full-fledged in the streets, and school was an after-thought, if that, except for a fashion show. See, I trick myself into believing that I didn't need to go to school. I mean why should I? I didn't need math because I knew how to count money. I didn't need social studies because I knew the history of the streets (so I thought). And science, why go there when I was a master chemist?

I'm pretty sure that it's needless to say that my mind was molested with these alien thoughts – almost in the same manner as the people of Sodom and Gomorrah 4000 years ago – and I now know this story is relevant to my history. I was once told before that if I looked hard enough, I would be able to find or see myself in the Bible and Quran. When I first heard this, I understood none of it and it floated to the back of my mind the same way the Titanic floated to the bottom of the sea, so yes, I can see myself in this story.

Those people had a diseased mind which manifested in their ways and actions. And the people of today have a dis-eased mind, but care not to recognize this, and I too, fit into this category. No wonder I struggled with changing my ways and actions up until the point when I just decided to let go of the past; meaning to stop making excuses for the reasons why my life is in such a debacle. I had a problem blaming my present life on my past. For everything I did, I would look back and say, *well this is the way I was raised*, and this thought is what kept me in the same mind frame as the dumb, deaf and blind. There's no way possible to hold on to your past life: people, places, and things; ideas, perspectives and/or understandings and expect to move forward in a positive manner. It took me a while to learn this, but now that I have it, I hope it's not too late!

In the story of Sodom and Gomorrah, God was going to destroy the city for their thoughts, actions and deeds, but he gave Lot, his wife and their children a way out. He made certain to say, to them (Gen. 19:17) 'TO NOT LOOK BACK' while you are fleeing from the city. But Lot's wife did look back and she died with the rest of the city - being turned into a pillar of salt. (Gen. 19:26)

I'm bringing this to your attention because it is pertinent to my life, but also to all of us as a whole. Where any and every time we choose to change our lives - fleeing as fast as possible from the destruction that once laid hold of us - we should do so without looking back/or holding on to anything in the past. While this may seem like nothing, it's probably the main reason why we're stuck where we are in life.

At least for me it is. I had to learn to not allow my past to be my excuse for my current situation; but also to never forget it and use the experience as learning tools to push me forward in life; to stop holding to my past. While this was the single hardest thing for me to accomplish – once it was done – my present and future became much clearer.

Peace

19

THE CLOSING

Oftentimes have I heard you speak of one who commits a wrong as though he were not one of you, but a stranger unto you and an intruder upon your world.

But I say that even as the holy and the righteous cannot rise beyond the highest which is in each one of you, So the wicked and the weak cannot fall lower than the lowest which is in you also.

And as a single leaf turns not yellow but with the silent knowledge of the whole tree, So the wrong-doer cannot do wrong without the hidden will of you all.

Like a procession you walk together towards your god-self. You are the way and the wayfarers. And when one of you falls down, he falls for those behind him, a caution against the stumbling stone. Ay, and he falls for those ahead of him, who though faster and surer of foot, yet removed not the stumbling stone.

And this also, though the word lie heavy upon your hearts:

The murdered is not unaccountable for his own murder,

And the robbed is not blameless in being robbed.

The righteous is not innocent of the deeds of the wicked,

And the white-handed is not clean in the doings of the felon.

Yea, the guilty is oftentimes the victim of the injured, and still more often the condemned is the burden bearer for the guiltless and unblamed.

You cannot separate the just from the unjust and the good from the wicked; For they stand together before the face of the sun even as the black thread and the white are woven together.

And when the black thread breaks the weaver shall look into the whole cloth, and he shall examine the loom also.

-Kahlil Gibran
"The Prophet"

BOOKS BY G. HOPKINS AND S. LITTLE

George Hopkins is the author of:

- On Time With Time
- Looking Up
- Like Petals to a Rose
- Petals
- The Long Way Home
- Pieces of a Dream
- The Victims
- You are who you are
- The Neverending Nightmare

Saleem Little is the Author of:

- Get In, Get Out
- Love and The Game
- Sincerely Yours (Trilogy)
- Crying for Tears
- G.O.D.: Gold, Oil & Drugs
- Special
- Naked
- The Muses of a Modern Mystic
- Apocrypha I & II
- Daydreams